Google Certified – Associate Cloud Engineer

Practice Questions
Version 1

www.ipspecialist.net

GCP Associate Cloud Engineer

Document Control

Proposal Name	:	GCP – Associate – Cloud Engineer – Practice Questions
Document Version	:	1.0
Document Release Date	:	24th June 2019

Copyright © 2018 IPSpecialist LTD.

Registered in England and Wales

Company Registration No: 10883539

Registration Office at: Office 32, 19-21 Crawford Street, London W1H 1PJ, United Kingdom

www.ipspecialist.net

All rights reserved. No part of this book may be reproduced or transmitted in any form or by any means, electronic or mechanical, including photocopying, recording, or by any information storage and retrieval system, without written permission from IPSpecialist LTD, except for the inclusion of brief quotations in a review.

Feedback:

If you have any comments regarding the quality of this book, or otherwise alter it to better suit your needs, you can contact us through email at info@ipspecialist.net

Please make sure to include the book title and ISBN in your message

About IPSpecialist

IPSPECIALIST LTD. IS COMMITTED TO EXCELLENCE AND DEDICATED TO YOUR SUCCESS.

Our philosophy is to treat our customers like family. We want you to succeed, and we are willing to do anything possible to help you make it happen. We have the proof to back up our claims. We strive to accelerate billions of careers with great courses, accessibility, and affordability. We believe that continuous learning and knowledge evolution are most important things to keep re-skilling and up-skilling the world.

Planning and creating a specific goal is where IPSpecialist helps. We can create a career track that suits your visions as well as develop the competencies you need to become a professional Network Engineer. We can also assist you with the execution and evaluation of proficiency level based on the career track you choose, as they are customized to fit your specific goals.

We help you STAND OUT from the crowd through our detailed IP training content packages.

Course Features:

- ❖ Self-Paced learning
  - Learn at your own pace and in your own time
- ❖ Covers Complete Exam Blueprint
  - Prep-up for the exam with confidence
- ❖ Case Study Based Learning
  - Relate the content with real life scenarios
- ❖ Subscriptions that suits you
  - Get more pay less with IPS Subscriptions
- ❖ Career Advisory Services
  - Let industry experts plan your career journey
- ❖ Virtual Labs to test your skills
  - With IPS vRacks, you can testify your exam preparations
- ❖ Practice Questions
  - Practice Questions to measure your preparation standards
- ❖ On Request Digital Certification
  - On request digital certification from IPSpecialist LTD

About the Authors:

This book has been compiled with the help of multiple professional engineers. These engineers specialize in different fields e.g Networking, Security, Cloud, Big Data, IoT etc. Each engineer develops content in its specialized field that is compiled to form a comprehensive certification guide.

About the Technical Reviewers:

Nouman Ahmed Khan

AWS-Architect, CCDE, CCIEX5 (R&S, SP, Security, DC, Wireless), CISSP, CISA, CISM is a Solution Architect working with a major telecommunication provider in Qatar. He works with enterprises, mega-projects, and service providers to help them select the best-fit technology solutions. He also works closely as a consultant to understand customer business processes and helps select an appropriate technology strategy to support business goals. He has more than 14 years of experience working in Pakistan/Middle-East & UK. He holds a Bachelor of Engineering Degree from NED University, Pakistan, and M.Sc. in Computer Networks from the UK.

Abubakar Saeed

Abubakar Saeed has more than twenty-five years of experience, Managing, Consulting, Designing, and implementing large-scale technology projects, extensive experience heading ISP operations, solutions integration, heading Product Development, Presales, and Solution Design. Emphasizing on adhering to Project timelines and delivering as per customer expectations, he always leads the project in the right direction with his innovative ideas and excellent management.

Syed Hanif Wasti

Syed Hanif Wasti is a Computer science graduate working professionally as a Technical Content Developer. He is a part of a team of professionals operating in the E-learning and digital education sector. He holds a bachelor's degree in Computer Sciences from PAF-KIET, Pakistan. He has completed training of MCP and CCNA. He has both technical knowledge and industry sounding information, which he uses efficiently in his career. He was working as a Database and Network administrator while having experience of software development.

Areeba Tanveer

Areeba Tanveer is working professionally as a Technical Content Developer. She holds Bachelor's of Engineering degree in Telecommunication Engineering from NED University of Engineering and Technology. She also worked as a project Engineer in Pakistan Telecommunication Company Limited (PTCL). She has both technical knowledge and industry sounding information, which she uses effectively in her career.

Afia Afaq

Afia Afaq works as a Technical Content Developer. She holds a Bachelor of Engineering Degree in Telecommunications Engineering from NED University of Engineering and Technology. She also has worked as an intern in Pakistan Telecommunication Company Limited (PTCL) as well as in Pakistan Meteorological Department (PMD). Afia Afaq uses her technical knowledge and industry sounding information efficiently in her career.

Hira Arif

Hira Arif is an Electrical Engineer Graduate from NED University of Engineering and Technology, working professionally as a Technical Content Writer. Prior to that, she worked as a Trainee Engineer at Sunshine Corporation. She utilizes her knowledge and technical skills profoundly when required.

Muhammad Yousuf

Muhammad Yousuf is a professional technical content writer. He is Certified Ethical Hacker (CEH) and Cisco Certified Network Associate (CCNA) in Routing and Switching, holding bachelor's degree in Telecommunication Engineering from Sir Syed University of Engineering and Technology. He has both technical knowledge and industry sounding information, which he uses perfectly in his career.

Free Resources:

With each workbook you buy from Amazon, IPSpecialist offers free resources to our valuable customers.

Once you buy this book you will have to contact us at support@ipspecialist.net or tweet @ipspecialistnet to get this limited time offer without any extra charges.

Free Resources Include:

Exam Practice Questions in Quiz Simulation: IP Specialists' Practice Questions have been developed keeping in mind the certification exam perspective. The collection of these questions from our technology workbooks is prepared to keep the exam blueprint in mind covering not only important but necessary topics as well. It is an ideal document to practice and revise your certification.

Career Report: This report is a step by step guide for a novice who wants to develop his/her career in the field of computer networks. It answers the following queries:

- Current scenarios and future prospects.
- Is this industry moving towards saturation or are new opportunities knocking at the door?
- What will the monetary benefits be?
- Why to get certified?
- How to plan and when will I complete the certifications if I start today?
- Is there any career track that I can follow to accomplish specialization level?

Furthermore, this guide provides a comprehensive career path towards being a specialist in the field of networking and also highlights the tracks needed to obtain certification.

Our Products

Technology Workbooks
IPSpecialist Technology workbooks are the ideal guides to developing the hands-on skills necessary to pass the exam. Our workbook covers official exam blueprint and explains the technology with real life case study based labs. The content covered in each workbook consists of individually focused technology topics presented in an easy-to-follow, goal-oriented, step-by-step approach. Every scenario features detailed breakdowns and thorough verifications to help you completely understand the task and associated technology.

We extensively used mind maps in our workbooks to visually explain the technology. Our workbooks have become a widely used tool to learn and remember the information effectively.

vRacks
Our highly scalable and innovative virtualized lab platforms let you practice the IP Specialist Technology Workbook at your own time and your own place as per your convenience.

Quick Reference Sheets
Our quick reference sheets are a concise bundling of condensed notes of the complete exam blueprint. It's an ideal handy document to help you remember the most important technology concepts related to certification exam.

Practice Questions
IP Specialists' Practice Questions are dedicatedly designed for certification exam perspective. The collection of these questions from our technology workbooks are prepared to keep the exam blueprint in mind covering not only important but necessary topics as well. It's an ideal document to practice and revise your certification.

Google Cloud Certifications

We will be discussing the general structure, basic stuff, advanced stuff and much more during the entire course. These things all-together make the foundation of Google Cloud, for your concepts building and your continuous learning. You are going to be challenged by Google in its exam to demonstrate what you have learned.

Logistics

In the exam, you have to answer 50 questions in 120 minutes, and its fee is USD 125 for each time you attempt it. Now, this is not something you can do online. You either have to appear in this exam at an authorized testing center, or you can give it on-site at Google Cloud Next. All of the questions in the exam will be in the form of Multiple Choice Questions (MCQs) with at least four options in each question. Also, some of the questions require multiple responses, for example, you may select 2 out of 5 options given in the questions.

If you fail the exam in the first attempt, you have to wait for 14 days and re-pay the full exam fee then retake the exam. If you are unable to pass the exam in the second attempt as well, then you have to wait for another 60 days for the third attempt. If you fail the exam even for the third time, then you have to wait for a whole year for another attempt.

One of the things you can do to check how much prepared you are for the exam is to take the official practice exam that Google offers. In this exam, you have got around 20 questions. This official practice exam is free to take because it is available online using a Google Forum based UI. This official practice exam is repeatable, and you can do it as many times as you want.

For the registration of your exam, you need to create a Web Assessor account with your email address. You can cancel or reschedule your exam without having to pay any extra fee before 72 hours of the exam. If you make changes within the 72 hours, it will cost some or maybe all of your exam fees. Remember to bring your IDs and your exam code which you get at the time of registration of the exam. During the exam, you can see there is an exam count down timer visible on every page, and you can flag any of the questions for later review. The overview page shows flags and lets you jump to any question. The responses can be changed until the exam ends. Double check your answers before moving on.

All GCP Certifications expire after two years. Re-certification expires two years after the renewal exam date, not the original date.

Quick Summary of the Exam

- Wide variety of Google Cloud services and their working. It focuses on IAM, Compute, Storage and also, a bit of network and data service is included.
- Covers Cloud SDK commands and Console operations which are required for day-to-day work. If you have not used GCP before, ensure that you do a lot of labs or else, you will be clueless about some of the questions and commands
- Tests are updated for the latest enhancements. There is no reference of Google Container Engine, and Google Kubernetes Engine, also covers Cloud Functions, and Cloud Spanner
- The list of topics is quite long, but some topics that you need to cover are General Services, Billing, Cloud SDK, Network Services, VPC, Load Balancer, Identity Service, Cloud IAM, Compute Services, GCE, Google AE, GKE, Storage Services, Cloud Storage, Cloud SQL, Cloud Spanner, BigQuery, Data Services, Google Stackdriver, DevOps Services, Deployment Manager and Cloud Launcher

Final Preparation

Let's discuss some exam tips. You will get several questions in exams on Kubernetes, and what happens when you deploy something on Kubernetes. You should be aware of the best practices for working with Google Cloud. Google has published valuable documents for the knowledge of Best Practices for Enterprise Organizations. This work book form IPSpecialist covers the whole exam blueprint and it will help you in getting familiar with IAM roles which describes the Cloud IAM roles that you grant to identities to access Cloud Platform resources. You should spend some time playing with the GCP Pricing Calculator. Several questions appear on how GCP Calculator works and understand the pricing structure of the different services. Several questions appear on how it works. Review gcloud structure before your exam. Another thing that comes up several times in the exam is Cloud Audit Logging.

Before the exam, re-read this exam guide and make sure you can do every task. Revise the key tips or exam tips provided in the course outline. Revise the key official documentation pages. Another important thing is to repeat the course practice exams because they are designed to identify your gaps and areas of weaknesses and research targets that matters. This is how you will understand the scenarios of the questions and suggest the best response. Go through the practice questions multiple times to make yourself ready for the exam.

You must identify the gaps and overcome those gaps by going through this exam guide, attempting the practice exams and reading of the student reports about their exams. Fill those gaps by going through our course, going through the official documentation, watching videos that Google has provided.

Soaring

Throughout the course, you will learn a lot of stuff which will prepare you for the exam. But, this is not the end; this is the beginning of your learning journey. You are going to take what you will learn into its practical use where you build a real system and teach your peers about it. The entire technology landscape has massively developed and expanded in the last 20 years; the technology will be better as the development occurs.

About Google Cloud Certifications

Google Cloud Platform (GCP) Certifications are industry-recognized credentials that validate your technical cloud skills and expertise while assisting you in your career growth. These are one of the most valuable IT certifications right now since GCP has established an overwhelming lead in the public cloud market. Even with the presence of several tough competitors such as Microsoft Azure, AWS, and Rackspace, GCP is gaining ground in the public cloud platform today, with an astounding collection of proprietary services that continues to grow.

The two key reasons as to why GCP certifications are prevailing in the current cloud-oriented job market:

- There is a dire need for skilled cloud engineers, developers, and architects – and the current shortage of experts is expected to continue into the foreseeable future.
- The Google Cloud Certified assignment means you've exhibited the important aptitudes to use Google Cloud innovation in a manner that can change organizations and definitively sway the general population and clients they serve.

Types of Certification

Role-based Certification

- Associate- Technical role-based certifications. No pre-requisite.
- Professional- Highest level technical role-based certification. Relevant Associate certification required

About GCP – Associate Cloud Engineer Exam

Exam Questions	Multiple choice and multiple answer
Number of Questions	50
Time to Complete	120 minutes
Available Languages	English, Japanese, Spanish, French, German, and Portuguese
Exam Fee	125 USD

The Google Certified Associate Cloud Engineer exam validates and individual's ability to deploy applications, monitor operations, and manage enterprise solutions. This individual is able to use GCP Console and the CLI to perform common platform-based tasks to maintain one or more deployed solutions that leverage Google-managed or self-managed services on Google Cloud. Example concepts you should understand for this exam include:

- Creation of projects and billing accounts
- Planning and configuring compute resources, data storage options, and network resources
- Deployment and implementation of a cloud solution
- Managing App Engine, Compute Engine, and Kubernetes Engine
- Management of IAM and Service accounts

Recommended Google Cloud Knowledge

- 6-month hands-on experience on Google Cloud Console and CLI
- Understanding of core GCP services and their uses
- This exam has no prerequisites

	Domain
Domain 1	Set up a cloud solution environment
Domain 2	Plan and configure a cloud solution
Domain 3	Deploy and implement a cloud solution
Domain 4	Ensure successful operation of a cloud solution
Domain 5	Configure access and security

Practice Questions

1. A Kubernetes Engine Cluster is created to deploy multiple Pods within the cluster. For later analysis, the container logs must be stored in BigQuery. By using Google recommended approaches, what will be the best solution? (Choose 2)
   A. Turn on Stackdriver Logging during the Kubernetes Engine cluster creation
   B. Turn on Stackdriver Monitoring during the Kubernetes Engine cluster creation
   C. Develop a custom add-on that uses Cloud Logging API and BigQuery API. Deploy the add-on to your Kubernetes Engine cluster
   D. Use the Stackdriver Logging export feature to create a sink to Cloud Storage. Create a Cloud Dataflow job that imports log files from Cloud Storage to BigQuery
   E. Use the Stackdriver Logging export feature to create a sink to BigQuery. Specify a filter expression to export log records related to your Kubernetes Engine cluster only

2. A new Compute Engine instance is created in us-central-1b zone. The data engineer requested to attach a GPU, but doing so is creating an error. What can be the cause of the error?
   A. Your instance isn't running with the correct scopes to allow GPUs
   B. The GPU is not supported for your OS
   C. Your instance isn't running with the default compute engine service account
   D. The desired GPU doesn't exist in that zone

3. It is necessary for a team to set up a MongoDB instance as quickly as possible, but you are unaware of how to install it and what configuration files are required. How can you overcome this problem?
   A. Use Cloud Memory store
   B. Learn and deploy MongoDB to a Compute Engine Instance
   C. Install with Cloud Launcher Marketplace
   D. Create a Deployment Manager template and deploy it.

4. Your billing branch has asked you to help them track spending towards a specific billing account. Billing branch has indicated that they prefer SQL querying to create their reports because they do not want to learn new tools. The data have to be as latest as possible. Which export alternative would work best for them?

Practice Questions

   A. File Export with JSON and load to Cloud SQL and provide Cloud SQL access to the billing department
   B. Create a sink to BigQuery and provide BigQuery access to the billing department
   C. Create a sink to Cloud SQL and provide Cloud SQL access to the billing department
   D. File Export with CSV and load to Cloud SQL and provide Cloud SQL access to the billing department

5. A team is working on designing an IoT solution. Several devices need to send data for processing in periodic time series. How can you ingest and store the data by using the GCP services?
   A. Pub/ Sub, Datastore
   B. Pub/ Sub, Dataproc
   C. Dataproc, Bigtable
   D. Pub/ Sub, Bigtable

6. An organization needs the logs from all applications, and they must be archived for ten years as part of their compliance. What would be the most feasible approach?
   A. Configure Stackdriver Monitoring for all Projects, and export to BigQuery
   B. Configure Stackdriver Monitoring for all Projects with the default retention policies
   C. Configure Stackdriver Monitoring for all Projects, and export to Google Cloud Storage
   D. Grant the security team access to the logs in each Project

7. Multiple applications are hosted on Compute Engine instances. And the company wants the instances to be resilient to any host maintenance activities which are performed on the instance. How can the instances be configured?
   A. Set automaticRestart availability policy to true
   B. Set automaticRestart availability policy to false
   C. Set onHostMaintenance availability policy to migrate instances
   D. Set onHostMaintenance availability policy to terminate instances

8. An App Engine Application is created in the us-central region, but the network team has configured all the VPN connections in asia-east2 region, which could not be moved. How can the location be changed efficiently?

Practice Questions

    A. Change the region in app.yaml and redeploy
    B. From the App Engine console, change the region of the application
    C. Change the region in application.xml within the application and redeploy
    D. Create a new project in the asia-east2 region and create an app engine in the project

9. Using principal of least privilege and permitting for maximum automation, what steps can you take to store audit logs for long-term access and to permit access for external auditors to view? (Choose 2)
    A. Generate a signed URL to the Stackdriver export destination for auditors to access
    B. Create an account for auditors to have view access to Stackdriver Logging
    C. Export audit logs to Cloud Storage via an export sink
    D. Export audit logs to BigQuery via an export sink

10. Your task supervisor wants to delegate the responsibility to upload items to Cloud storage buckets for his team members. Considering the principle of least privilege, which function you assign to the team members?
    A. roles/storage.objectAdmin
    B. roles/storage.objectViewer
    C. roles/storage.objectCreator
    D. roles/storage.admin

11. Your billing department has requested you to help them track spending against a specific billing account. They have indicated that they choose to use Excel to create their reports, so they do not want to learn new tools. Which export option would work best for them?
    A. BigQuery Export
    B. File Export with JSON
    C. SQL Export
    D. File Export with CSV

12. A Cloud Storage bucket is required to host static web assets with dozens of HTML pages, some Javascript files, and CSS. How can you make the bucket public?
    A. Check the "make public" box on the GCP Console for the bucket
    B. gsutil iam ch allAuthenticatedUsers:objectViewer gs://bucket-name
    C. gsutil make-public gs://bucket-name

Practice Questions

D. gsutil iam ch allUsers:objectViewer gs://bucket-name

13. You require an instance template which contains a web application. You need to deploy the application so that it can be scaled based on the HTTP traffic it receives. What should you do?
    A. Create a VM from the instance template. Create a custom image from the VM's disk. Export the image to Cloud Storage. Create an HTTP load balancer and add the Cloud Storage bucket as its backend service
    B. Create an unmanaged instance group based on the instance template. Configure autoscaling based on HTTP traffic and configure the instance group as the backend service of an HTTP load balancer
    C. Create a managed instance group based on the instance template. Configure autoscaling based on HTTP traffic and configure the instance group as the backend service of an HTTP load balancer
    D. Create the necessary number of instances required for peak user traffic based on the instance template. Create an unmanaged instance group and add the instances to that instance group. Configure the instance group as the Backend Service of an HTTP load balancer

14. Production and Test environment is set up by a company because they want to use different subjects. The key requirement is that the VMs can communicate with each other using internal IPs and no additional routes are configured. Prescribed the best solution?
    A. Configure a single VPC with two subnets having the same CIDR range hosted in the same region
    B. Configure a single VPC with two subnets having the different CIDR range hosted in the different region
    C. Configure 2 VPCs with one subnet each having the same CIDR range hosted in the same region
    D. Configure 2 VPCs with one subnet each having the different CIDR range hosted in the different region

15. An application is running on a machine type having two virtual CPUs and 4GB RAM, but there have been plenty of memory problems. How can you increase the memory of the application with minimal downtime?
    A. In GCP console, upgrade the memory of the Compute Engine instance
    B. Use gcloud compute instances increase-memory to increase the memory

C. Use Live migration to move to machine type with higher memory
D. Use Live migration to move to machine type with higher CPU

16. You have been tasked to grant access to sensitive files to external auditors for a limited period of four hours only. The files should not be strictly available after four hours. Adhering to Google best practices, how could you efficiently share the document?
   A. Host a website on Compute Engine instance and expose the files using Public DNS and share the URL with the auditors. Bring down the instance after 4 hours
   B. Host a website on App Engine instance and expose the files using Public DNS and share the URL with the auditors. Bring down the instance after 4 hours
   C. Store the file in Cloud Storage. Generate a signed URL with 4 hours expiry and share it with the auditors
   D. Store the file in Cloud Storage. Grant the allUsers access to the file share it with the auditors. Remove allUsers access after 4 hours

17. You work on a project with two compliance necessities. The primary requirement is that your developers should be capable of seeing the GCP billing charges for their projects only. The second requirement describes that your finance team members can set budgets and view the current costs for all projects within the organization. The finance team should no longer be able to view the project contents. You need to set permissions. What must you do?
   A. Add the finance team members to the default IAM Owner role. Add the developers to a custom role that allows them to see their own spend only
   B. Add the finance team members to the Billing Administrator role for each of the billing accounts that they need to manage. Add the developers to the Viewer role for the Project
   C. Add the developers and finance managers to the Viewer role for the Project
   D. Add the finance team to the Viewer role for the Project. Add the developers to the Security Reviewer role for each of the billing accounts

18. Security Team wants to audit network traffic within the network. What is the easiest way to ensure that they have access to the data they require?
   A. Disable Flow Logs.
   B. Enable Flow Logs.
   C. Enable VPC Network Logs.

Practice Questions

   D. Add a firewall capture filter.

19. Your company has a set of compute engine instances that could be hosting production-based applications. These applications might be running 24x7 throughout the year. You want to implement the cost-effective, scalable and high availability solution even if a zone fails. How would you design the solution?
   A. Use Managed instance groups with pre-emptible instances across multiple zones
   B. Use Managed instance groups across multiple zones
   C. Use managed instance groups with instances in a single zone
   D. Use Unmanaged instance groups across multiple zones

20. You are creating a single pre-emptible VM instance named "preempt" for use as scratch space for a single workload. In case your VM is pre-empted, you want to make sure that disk contents can be re-used. Which gcloud command would you use to create this instance?
   A. gcloud compute instances create "preempt" --preemptible --no-boot-disk-auto-delete
   B. gcloud compute instances create "preempt" --preemptible --boot-disk-auto-delete-no
   C. gcloud compute instances create "preempt" –preemptible
   D. gcloud compute instances create "preempt" --no-auto-delete

21. A company is hosting their static website on Cloud Storage, and you implemented a change to add PDF files to the website. When the user clicks the PDF files, it downloads the PDF instead of opening it the browser. How can you fix this issue?
   A. Set content-type as object metadata to application/octet-stream on the files
   B. Set content-type as object metadata to application/pdf on the files
   C. Set content-type as object metadata to application/octet-stream on the bucket
   D. Set content-type as object metadata to application/pdf on the bucket

22. You are informed that one of the projects using the old billing account. How can you resolve this problem?
   A. Go to the Project page; expand the Billing tile; select the Billing Account option; select the correct billing account and save
   B. Go to the Billing page; view the list of projects; find the project in question and select Change billing account; select the correct billing account and save
   C. Delete the project and recreate it with the correct billing account

D. Submit a support ticket requesting the change.

23. A SysOps admin configured a lifecycle rule on an object versioning enabled multi-regional bucket. Which of the following statement effect reflects the following lifecycle config?

{ "rule": [{ "action": {"type": "Delete"}, "condition": {"age": 30, "isLive": false} }, { "action": {"type": "SetStorageClass", "storageClass": "COLDLINE"}, "condition": {"age": 365, "matchesStorageClass": "MULTI_REGIONAL"} }] }

   A. Archive objects older than 30 days and moves objects to Coldline Storage after 365 days if the storage class in Multi-regional
   B. Delete objects older than 30 days and move objects to Coldline Storage after 365 days if the storage class in Multi-regional
   C. Delete archived objects older than 30 days and move objects to Coldline Storage after 365 days if the storage class in Multi-regional
   D. Move objects to Coldline Storage after 365 days if the storage class in Multi-Regional First rule does not affect the bucket

24. You have to test out the latest version of MS SQL on windows instance. You have created a VM and need to connect into the instance. Which of the step is followed to connect to the instance?
   A. Generate a Windows password in the console, then use a client capable of communicating via RDP and provide the credentials
   B. Generate a Windows password in the console, and then use the RDP button to connect in through the console
   C. Connect in with your own RDP client using your Google Cloud username and password
   D. From the console click the SSH button to connect automatically

25. An App Engine Application is serving as front-end and going to publish messages to Pub/ Sub. But the Pub/ Sub API has not been enabling yet. How can the API be enabled?
   A. Use a service account with the Pub/Sub Admin role to auto-enable the API
   B. Enable the API in the Console
   C. Application's in App Engine don't require external APIs to be enabled
   D. The API will be enabled the first time the code attempts to access Pub/Sub

26. Cloud SQL is used by a company to host critical data. If a complete zone goes down, they want to enable the high availability for this case. How can you configure this?
    A. Create a Read replica in the same region different zone
    B. Create a Read replica in the different region different zone
    C. Create a Failover replica in the same region different zone
    D. Create a Failover replica in the different region different zone

27. You've set up an instance inside your new network and subnet. You create firewall rules to target all instances in your network with the following firewall rules.

| NAME:open-ssh | NETWORK:devnet | DIRECTION:INGRESS | PRIORITY:1000 | ALLOW:tcp:22   NAME:deny-all | NETWORK:devnet | DIRECTION:INGRESS | PRIORITY:5000 | DENY:tcp:0-65535,udp:0-6553 |

   If you try to SSH to the instance, what would be the result?
    A. SSH would be denied and would need gcloud firewall refresh command for the allow rule to take effect
    B. SSH would be allowed as the allow rule overrides the deny
    C. SSH would be denied as the deny rule overrides the allow
    D. SSH would be denied and would need instance reboot for the to allow rule to take effect

28. A data team is working on some new machine learning models, and they are generating multiple files per day and want to store them in the regional bucket. Their major focus is the files of the last week, but they want to store all the files to keep safe if needed. How can you lower the storage cost?
    A. Create a Cloud Function triggered when objects are added to a bucket. Look at the date on all the files and move it to Nearline storage if it's older than a week
    B. Create a Cloud Function triggered when objects are added to a bucket. Look at the date on all the files and move it to Coldline storage if it's older than a week
    C. Create a lifecycle policy to switch the objects older than a week to Coldline storage
    D. Create a lifecycle policy to switch the objects older than a week to Nearline storage

29. A company requires to host confidential documents in Cloud Storage. The data must be highly available and resilient in case of a regional outage, as per the compliance requirement. Which of the following storage classes meet the requirement? (Choose 2)

Practice Questions

A. Standard
B. Regional
C. Coldline
D. Dual-Regional
E. Multi-Regional

30. To verify the assigned permission in custom IAM role, what should you do?
    A. Use the GCP Console, IAM section to view the information
    B. Use the gcloud init command to view the information
    C. Use the GCP Console, Security section to view the information
    D. Use the GCP Console, API section to view the information

31. A company is needed to set up a template for deploying resources. They want the dynamic provisioning with the specifications in the configured files. Which of the following service is ideal for this requirement?
    A. Cloud Composer
    B. Deployment Manager
    C. Cloud Scheduler
    D. Cloud Deployer

32. By using principal of least privilege and allowing max automation, what steps you are taking to store audit logs for long-term access and to permit access for external auditors to view? (Choose 2)
    A. Create an account for auditors to have view access to Stackdriver Logging
    B. Export audit logs to Cloud Storage via an export sink
    C. Export audit logs to BigQuery via an export sink
    D. Create an account for auditors to have view access to export storage bucket with the Storage Object Viewer role.

33. A company wants to set up a VPC network, and they want to configure a single subnet within the VPC with maximum range. What is most preferred CIDR block?
    A. 0.0.0.0/0
    B. 10.0.0.0/8
    C. 172.16.0.0/12
    D. 192.168.0.0/16

21

34. In order to find out the owner access of the project named "My Project" what should you do?
    A. In the Google Cloud Platform Console, go to the IAM page for your organization and apply the filter "Role: Owner."
    B. In the Google Cloud Platform Console, go to the IAM page for your project and apply the filter "Role: Owner."
    C. Use gcloud iam list-grantable-role --project my-project from your Terminal
    D. Use gcloud iam list-grantable-role from Cloud Shell on the project page

35. A solution is created to remove backup files which are older than 90 days from the backup Cloud Storage bucket. And you want to optimize ongoing Cloud storage spend. What should you do?
    A. Write a lifecycle management rule in JSON and push it to the bucket with gsutil
    B. Schedule a cron script using gsutil ls –lr gs://backups/** to find and remove items older than 90 days
    C. Schedule a cron script using gsutil ls –l gs://backups/** to find and remove items older than 90 days and schedule it with cron
    D. Write a lifecycle management rule in XML and push it to the bucket with gsutil

36. The development team has asked you to set up an external TCP load balancer with SSL offload. Prescribe the load balancer which can be used?
    A. SSL Proxy
    B. HTTP Load Balancer
    C. TCP Proxy
    D. HTTPS Load Balancer

37. A company demands to create a new Kubernetes cluster on GCP, and they want to upgrade the nodes to the latest stable version of Kubernetes with no manual intervention, for security purpose. How can you have configured the Kubernetes cluster?
    A. Always use the latest version while creating the cluster
    B. Enable node auto-repairing
    C. Enable node auto-upgrades
    D. Apply security patches on the nodes as they are released

38. A company wants to reduce the cost of infrequently accessed data by transferring it to the cloud. But the data can still be accessed once a month to refresh historical charts. And the data longer than 5years are no longer needed. How can you manage and store the data?
   A. In Google Cloud Storage and stored in a Multi-Regional bucket. Set an Object Lifecycle Management policy to delete data older than five years
   B. In Google Cloud Storage and stored in a Multi-Regional bucket. Set an Object Lifecycle Management policy to change the storage class to Coldline for data older than five years
   C. In Google Cloud Storage and stored in a Nearline bucket. Set an Object Lifecycle Management policy to delete data older than five years
   D. In Google Cloud Storage and stored in a Nearline bucket. Set an Object Lifecycle Management policy to change the storage class to Coldline for data older than five years

39. Some updates for an application is created working on App Engine, and you want to deploy the updates without disturbing your users. You must be rolled back as soon as possible if it fails. How can you perform this?
   A. Delete the current version of your application. Deploy the update using the same version identifier as the deleted version
   B. Notify your users of an upcoming maintenance window. Deploy the update in that maintenance window
   C. Deploy the update as the same version that is currently running
   D. Deploy the update as a new version. Migrate traffic from the current version to the new version

40. A new application for App Engine is developed and is ready to deploy it to the production. You have to estimate the cost of running an application on GCP as quickly as possible. How can you achieve this?
   A. Create a YAML file with the expected usage. Pass this file to the gcloud app estimate command to get an accurate estimation
   B. Multiply the costs of your application when it was in development by the number of expected users to get an accurate estimation
   C. Use the pricing calculator for App Engine to get an accurate estimation of the expected charges
   D. Create a ticket with Google Cloud Billing Support to get an accurate estimation

Practice Questions

41. An application is on GAE which is serving production traffic. You are going to deploy a risky but necessary change to the application. It can take down your service if it is not coded properly and you realize that it can only be tested properly by live user traffic. How can you test the feature?
    A. Deploy the new application version temporarily, and then roll it back
    B. Create a second project with the new app in isolation, and onboard users
    C. Set up a second Google App Engine service, and then update a subset of clients to hit the new service
    D. Deploy a new version of the application, and use traffic splitting to send a small percentage of traffic to it

42. A company has a mission-critical application that serves its user globally. You need to select the relational and transactional data storage system for the application. Which product should you prescribe? (Choose 2)
    A. BigQuery
    B. Cloud SQL
    C. Cloud Spanner
    D. Cloud Bigtable
    E. Cloud Datastore

43. You are required to create new Kubernetes cluster, which can auto-scale the number of worker nodes on GCP. How should you do?
    A. Create a cluster on Kubernetes Engine and enable autoscaling on Kubernetes Engine
    B. Create a cluster on Kubernetes Engine and enable autoscaling on the instance group of the cluster
    C. Configure a Compute Engine instance as a worker and add it to an unmanaged instance group. Add a load balancer to the instance group and rely on the load balancer to create additional Compute Engine instances when needed
    D. Create Compute Engine instances for the workers and the master and install Kubernetes. Rely on Kubernetes to create additional Compute Engine instances when needed.

44. A new development Kubernetes cluster needs to be created with three nodes. The cluster will be named as project-1-cluster. Which command can create a cluster?

Practice Questions

  A. gcloud container clusters create project-1-cluster --num-nodes 3
  B. kubectl clusters create project-1-cluster 3
  C. kubectl clusters create project-1-cluster --num-nodes 3
  D. gcloud container clusters create project-1-cluster 3

45. An on-premise application is migrating to Google Cloud. The application is using a component with requires a licensing server. The license server contains the IP address10.28.0.10. You need to deploy the application without making any changes in the code or configuration. How can you deploy the application?
   A. Create a subnet with a CIDR range of 10.28.0.0/28. Reserve a static internal IP address of 10.28.0.10. Assign the static address to the license server instance
   B. Create a subnet with a CIDR range of 10.28.0.0/28. Reserve a static external IP address of 10.28.0.10. Assign the static address to the license server instance
   C. Create a subnet with a CIDR range of 10.28.0.0/28. Reserve an ephemeral internal IP address of 10.28.0.10. Assign the static address to the license server instance
   D. Create a subnet with a CIDR range of 10.28.0.0/28. Reserve an ephemeral external IP address of 10.28.0.10. Assign the static address to the license server instance

46. You have to get all of your team's public SSH keys onto a specific Bastion Host instance of a particular project. You have collected all of them. What is the best way to get the keys deployed?
   A. Add all of the keys into a file that's formatted according to the requirements. Use the gcloud compute instances add-metadata command to upload the keys to each instance
   B. Add all of the keys into a file that's formatted according to the requirements. Use the gcloud compute project-info add-metadata command to upload the keys
   C. Use the gcloud compute ssh command to upload all the keys
   D. Format all of the keys as needed and then, using the user interface, upload each key one at a time

47. Bob wants to be able to create a new instance on Compute Engine project named as Project A by using the principle of least privilege. How can you give him access without providing much more permissions?
   A. Give Bob Compute Engine Admin Role for Project A.
   B. Create a shared VPC that Bob can access Compute resources from.
   C. Give Bob Project Editor IAM role for Project A.

25

Practice Questions

D. Give Bob Compute Engine Instance Admin Role for Project A.

48. Project owner and co-workers are required to deploy a new version of an application on App Engine. You need to follow Google recommended practices. Which IAM role should you grant to your co-workers?
    A. Project Editor
    B. App Engine Service Admin
    C. App Engine Deployer
    D. App Engine Code Viewer

49. You have set up and tested several custom roles in your development project. How can you create the same roles for the new projects in the fastest way?
    A. Recreate them in the new project
    B. Use the gcloud iam copy roles command and set the destination project
    C. In GCP console, select the roles and click the Export button
    D. Use the gcloud iam roles copy command and set the destination project

50. You are writing an application on Python and demands that your application runs on a sandboxed managed environment with the capability to scale up in seconds for huge spikes in demand. On which service you host your application?
    A. Compute Engine
    B. App Engine Flexible Environment
    C. Kubernetes Engine
    D. App Engine Standard Environment

51. You have a file of 20 GB that you have to share with some contractors securely. They need it as quickly as they can. How fast and secure would they get the file?
    A. Upload the file to Cloud Storage. Grant the allAuthenticated users token view permissions.
    B. Upload the file to Bigtable using the bulk data import tool. Then provide the contractors with read access to the database.
    C. Using composite objects and parallel uploads to upload the file to Cloud Storage quickly. Then generate a signed URL and securely share it with the contractors.
    D. Set up a VPC with a custom subnet. Create a subnet tunnel. Upload the file to a network share. Grant the contractor's temporary access.

Practice Questions

52. The test suite of your company is a custom C++ application running tests on virtual Linux machines every day. The whole test suite is completed for several hours and runs on a limited number of test servers on the premises. Your company would like to move the testing infrastructure to the cloud to reduce the time it takes to fully test the system change while minimizing tests. What should you recommend cloud infrastructure?
    A. Google App Engine with Google Stackdriver for logging.
    B. Google Cloud Dataproc to run Apache Hadoop jobs to process each test.
    C. Google Compute Engine unmanaged instance groups and Network Load Balancer.
    D. Google Compute Engine managed instance groups with auto-scaling.

53. An organization plans to migrate its web app to Google App Engine, and they still want to use the on-site database. How can the application be configured?
    A. Setup the application using App Engine Flexible environment with Cloud VPN to connect to database
    B. Setup the application using App Engine Flexible environment with Cloud Router to connect to database
    C. Setup the application using App Engine Standard environment with Cloud Router to connect to database
    D. Setup the application using App Engine Standard environment with Cloud VPN to connect to database

54. A company has new features that you want to slowly implement in order to monitor for errors. The change includes some major changes to the UI. In order to perform a canary operation, you opted to use traffic splitting. You will begin by rolling the code out to 15% of your users. How do you manage the same experience with setting up traffic splits?
    A. Deploy the new version using the no-promote flag. Split the traffic using a random distribution.
    B. Deploy the new version using the no-promote flag. Split the traffic using Cookie.
    C. Use the gcloud app deploy command with the distribution flag to deploy and split the traffic in one command.
    D. Deploy the new version. Split the traffic using an IP or cookie based distribution.

55. An organization handles large volumes of time-stamped IoT data. There can be several petabytes of total data volume. The data must be written and modified at high

speed. The most efficient storage option for your data is to be used. What product are you supposed to use?

A. BigQuery
B. Cloud Bigtable
C. Cloud Storage
D. Cloud Data

56. The infrastructure for the new application is planned by a company which has to store more than 100 TB or a petabyte of information in NoSQL format to be read / write low latency and high-performance analytics. How should you use the storage option?

A. Cloud Spanner
B. Cloud Datastore
C. Cloud Bigtable
D. Cloud SQL

57. You have used the gcloud app deployment for App Engine. However, you do not find the implementation for the intended project, and the application seems to have been deployed in the wrong project. How can you find out which project was used for the application?

A. Check index.yaml for the project
B. Check application web.xml for the project
C. Check app.yaml for the project
D. Run gcloud config list to check for the project

58. Your firm designs a Cloud Spanner interacting application. You should view and edit the Cloud Spanner tables in the application. In view of the lower privilege principle, what role should you give the team members?

A. roles/spanner.databaseAdmin
B. roles/spanner.databaseReader
C. roles/spanner.databaseUser
D. roles/spanner.viewer

59. In Google Cloud Storage, your company collects and stores security camera footage. In the first 30 days, threat detection, object detection, trend analysis, and suspicious behavior detection are regularly processed with footages. All data storage costs should be reduced to a minimum then how are the videos to store?

A. Use Google Cloud Regional Storage for the first 30 days, and then move to Google Persistent Disk.
B. Use Google Cloud Nearline Storage for the first 30 days, and then move to Coldline Storage.
C. Use Google Cloud Regional Storage for the first 30 days, and then move to Nearline Storage.
D. Use Google Cloud Regional Storage for the first 30 days, and then move to Coldline Storage.

60. With 30 microservices, a company is developing a large distributed application. they must connect to a back-end database for each of distributed microservices. The credentials should be safely stored. Where are the credentials to be stored?
    A. In a config file that has restricted access through ACLs
    B. In a secret management system
    C. In an environment variable
    D. In the source code

61. In the European-West1 region, organization project has all its computer engine resources. The default region for gcloud commands is Europa-west1. What are they supposed to do?
    A. Create a VPN from on-premises to a subnet in Europe-west1, and use that connection when executing gcloud commands.
    B. Use Cloud Shell instead of the command line interface of your device. Launch Cloud Shell after you navigate to a resource in the Europe-west1 region. The Europe-west1 region will automatically become the default region.
    C. Use gcloud config set compute/region europe-west1 to set the default region for future gcloud commands.
    D. Use gcloud config set compute/zone europe-west1 to set the default region for future gcloud commands.

62. A company created a cluster called "ips" of the Kubernetes engine that has the cluster pool named "pri-node pool." Now they have realized that in order to meet the capacity requirements between 10 and 20, they need more total nodes. What is the command to change its pool's number of nodes?
    A. gcloud container clusters resize ips --node pool 'pri-node-pool' --size 20
    B. kubectl container clusters update ips --node pool 'pri-node-pool' --num-nodes 20

C. gcloud container clusters update ips --node pool 'pri-node-pool' --num-nodes 20

D. gcloud container clusters resize ips --node pool 'pri-node-pool' --num-nodes 20

63. Auditors visit their team every 12 months to review any policy changes made during the previous 12 months by Google Cloud Identity and Access Management (Cloud IAM). The process of analysis and audit will be streamlined and expedited. What should you do?

    A. Enable Google Cloud Storage (GCS) log export to audit logs into a GCS bucket and delegate access to the bucket
    B. Use Cloud Functions to transfer log entries to Google Cloud SQL and use ACLs and views to limit an auditor's view
    C. Enable Logging export to Google BigQuery and use ACLs and views to scope the data shared with the auditor
    D. Create custom Google Stackdriver alerts and send them to the auditor

64. You have a cloud storage bucket, which has a dozen HTML pages, a few JavaScript file, and a certain CSS to hold static web assets. How can you publicize the bucket?

    A. gsutil make-public gs://bucket-name
    B. Set allUsers to have the Storage Object Viewer role.
    C. Check the "make public" box on the GCP Console for the bucket
    D. Set allAuthenticatedUsers to have the Storage Object Viewer role.

65. The media files that you have to migrate to Google Cloud Storage are more than 100 GB each. The files are in the data center on site. How can you migrate to speed up the transfer process?

    A. Start a recursive upload.
    B. Use the Cloud Transfer Service to transfer.
    C. Use parallel uploads to break the file into smaller chunks then transfer it simultaneously.
    D. Use multi-threaded uploads using the -m option.

66. A leading software engineer says his new app design is using web sockets and HTTP sessions not distributed across web servers. You want to support him in making sure the Google Cloud Platform app is running correctly. What are you supposed to do?

    A. Help the engineer redesign the application to use a distributed user session service that does not rely on WebSockets and HTTP sessions.

B. Meet with the cloud operations team and the engineer to discuss load balancer options.
C. Review the encryption requirements for WebSocket connections with the security team.
D. Help the engineer to convert his WebSocket code to use HTTP streaming.

67. A new firewall rule has been developed to allow traffic entering port 22 using a "dev-ssh" target tag. You have tried, and you are still unable to connect to one of your instances. How you resolve this issue?
    A. Apply a network tag of "dev-ssh" to the instance you're trying to connect into and test again.
    B. Reboot the instances for the firewall rule to take effect.
    C. Use source tags in place of the target tags.
    D. Run the gcloud firewall-rules refresh command, as they need to reload

68. An organization transfers its business applications to Google Cloud. Their security team wishes to see every project in the organization in detail. The Google Cloud Resource Manager is provided by cloud engineer and set up the CEO as the org admin. What roles should you give the security team to Google Cloud Identity and Access Management?
    A. Project owner, network admin
    B. Org admin, project browser
    C. Org viewer, project viewer
    D. Org viewer, the project owner

69. How you estimate the annual cost of running a nightly BigQuery query?
    A. Use bq query --dry_run to determine the number of bytes read by the query. Use this number in the Pricing Calculator.
    B. Use bq estimate to determine the amount billed for a single query. Multiply this amount by 365.
    C. Use gcloud query --dry_run to determine the number of bytes read by the query. Use this number in the Pricing Calculator.
    D. Use gcloud estimate to determine the amount billed for a single query. Multiply this amount by 365.

Practice Questions

70. You have used a Deployment Manager application. The deployment should be updated with minimum downtime. How can you do this?
    A. gcloud deployment-manager resources update
    B. gcloud deployment-manager resources create
    C. gcloud deployment-manager deployments update
    D. gcloud deployment-manager deployments create

71. You are payable for your two projects via a self-served billing account. Your billing threshold is $1000,00, and you spend about $50 a day between the two projects. You have been accused for the last 18 days. Where are you going to be charged next given the above data?
    A. In 12 days, making it 30 days since the previous payment.
    B. In 2 days when you'll hit your billing threshold.
    C. On the first day of the next month.
    D. On the thirtieth day of the month.

72. A firm is hosting critical data by using Cloud SQL. You want to make it possible to recover Point In Time (PIT) to a particular point in for instance. How are you to set up the same thing?
    A. Enable Binary logging and backups for the instance
    B. Create a Failover replica for the instance
    C. Switch to Spanner 3 node cluster
    D. Create a Read replica for the instance

73. It was your task to get all public SSH keys of your team into all instances of a particular project. You gathered all of them. What is the easiest way to deploy the keys?
    A. Format all of the keys as needed and then, using the user interface, upload each key one at a time.
    B. Use the gcloud compute ssh command to upload all the keys
    C. Add all of the keys into a file that's formatted according to the requirements. Use the gcloud compute project-info add-metadata command to upload the keys.
    D. Add all of the keys into a file that's formatted according to the requirements. Use the gcloud compute instances add-metadata command to upload the keys to each instance

Practice Questions

74. An organization have hardcoded the database credentials to be used by application on Kubernetes Engine. The YAML they're using looks similar to the following:apiVersion: "extensions/v1beta1" kind: "Deployment" metadata: name: "products-service" namespace: "default" labels: app: "products-service" spec: replicas: 3 selector: matchLabels: app: "products-service" template: metadata: labels: app: "products-service" spec: containers: - name: "products" image: "gcr.io/find-seller-app-dev/products:latest" env: - name: "database_user" value: "admin" - name: "database_password" value: "TheB3stP@ssWord" What is Google's recommended best practice for working with sensitive information inside of Kubernetes?

    A. Store the credentials in a Secret.
    B. Use an environment variable.
    C. Mount the credentials in a volume.
    D. Store the credentials in a ConfigMap.

75. Your company wishes to host its confidential documents in Cloud Storage. Due to compliance requirements, data are necessary even in case of a regional failure to be highly available and resilient. What classes of storage help meet the needs? (select any 2)

    A. Standard
    B. Nearline
    C. Regional
    D. Dual regional
    E. Multi-regional

76. In your new network and subnet, you have set up an instance. Your firewall rules shall be used for all instances in your network with the following firewall rules. NAME:deny-all | NETWORK:devnet | DIRECTION:INGRESS | PRIORITY:1000 | DENY:tcp:0-65535,udp:0-6553 NAME:open-ssh | NETWORK:devnet | DIRECTION:INGRESS | PRIORITY:5000 | ALLOW:tcp:22. When you try to connect to the instance via SSH, you get connection timeout. What was the issue behind this?

    A. SSH would be denied as the deny rule overrides the allow
    B. Firewall rule needs to be applied to the instance specifically.
    C. The SSH key hasn't been uploaded to the instance.
    D. SSH would be denied and would need instance reboot for the to allow rule to take effect

Practice Questions

77. A company has a managed automatic instance group set to scale based on the 60 percent CPU usage. In the instance group, there are currently 3 instances. The CPU usage is 70 percent, of the instance they are logged in. The instance group does not, however, start another instance. What is the most probable reason for this?
   A. The load balancer doesn't recognize the instance as healthy.
   B. The autoscaler takes 60 seconds before creating a new instance.
   C. The average CPU for the entire instance group is below 60%.
   D. The autoscaler is disabled.

78. App Engine applications have been running for a few weeks in a standard environment. You just deployed a broken version with a number of successful deployments, and the developers are not available. What is the quickest way to get the site to work?
   A. In GCP console, click the Rollback button on the versions page.
   B. In GCP console, click Traffic Splitting and direct 100% of the traffic to the previous version.
   C. Use the gcloud app deployments rollback command.
   D. Use the gcloud app deployments revert command.

79. An enterprise has created a new account and must transfer the projects to the account for payments. What role does the billing account need to change? (select any 2)
   A. Project Editor
   B. Billing Account Manager
   C. Billing Account Billing administrator
   D. Project Billing manager
   E. Project Owner

80. Company moves its storage to Google Cloud Storage (GCS). The data includes personal data (PII) and customer information sensitive. How should you use a security strategy for GCS?
   A. Create randomized bucket and object names. Enable public access, but only provide specific file URLs to people who do not have Google accounts and need access.
   B. Grant no Google Cloud Identity and Access Management (Cloud IAM) roles to users, and use granular ACLs on the bucket.
   C. Grant IAM read-only access to users, and use default ACLs on the bucket.

D. Use signed URLs to generate time-bound access to objects.

81. In the European-west1-d zone, you have an application server running on Compute Engine. You must ensure high availability and replicate the server with the minimum possible steps to the European-West2-C area. How you can do this?
    A. Use gcloud compute instances move with parameter --destination-zone europe-west2-c to move the instance to the new zone.
    B. Use "gcloud" to copy the disk to the europe-west2-c zone. Create a new VM with that disk.
    C. Create a snapshot from the disk. Create a disk from the snapshot in the europe-west1-d zone and then move the disk to europe-west2-c. Create a new VM with that disk.
    D. Create a snapshot from the disk. Create a disk from the snapshot in the europe-west2-c zone. Create a new VM with that disk.

82. An organization decided to store Cloud Storage data files. To begin with, the information would be host in a regional bucket. To move the data for archiving after 30 days and delete it after one year, you need to configure the Cloud Storage Lifecycle rule. What should you do with these two actions?
    A. Create a Cloud Storage lifecycle rule with Age: "30", Storage Class: "Standard", and Action: "Set to Nearline", and create a second GCS life-cycle rule with Age: "275", Storage Class: "Nearline", and Action: "Delete".
    B. Create a Cloud Storage lifecycle rule with Age: "30", Storage Class: "Standard", and Action: "Set to Nearline", and create a second GCS life-cycle rule with Age: "365", Storage Class: "Nearline", and Action: "Delete".
    C. Create a Cloud Storage lifecycle rule with Age: "30", Storage Class: "Standard", and Action: "Set to Coldline", and create a second GCS life-cycle rule with Age: "275", Storage Class: "Coldline", and Action: "Delete".
    D. Create a Cloud Storage lifecycle rule with Age: "30", Storage Class: "Standard", and Action: "Set to Coldline", and create a second GCS life-cycle rule with Age: "365", Storage Class: "Coldline", and Action: "Delete".

83. A company is hosting critical data with Cloud SQL. If you have a complete zone failure, then you high availability. How you can do this?
    A. Create a Failover replica in the different region different zone
    B. Create a Failover replica in the same region different zone

C. Create a Read replica in the different region different zone

D. Create a Read replica in the same region different zone

84. The company wants to build a Cloud storage bucket application that stores the images, generates thumbnails and resizes the images. They want to use a managed service that automatically helps you scale from 0 to scale and back to 0. Which GCP service meets the needs?
    A. Cloud Functions
    B. Google App Engine
    C. Google Kubernetes Engine
    D. Google Compute Engine

85. The new Jenkins instance must need to be set up quickly. How you can do this?
    A. Create a Deployment Manager template and deploy it.
    B. Install with Cloud Launcher
    C. Deploy the jar file to a Compute Engine instance.
    D. Use Google's Managed Jenkins Service.

86. You work in a small company where all the resources of a given project can be viewed. You would like to give them access to the recommended practices of Google. How you do this?
    A. Create a new Google Group and add all members to the group. Use gcloud iam roles create with the Project Viewer role and Group email address.
    B. Create a script that uses gcloud iam roles create for all users' email addresses and the Project Viewer role.
    C. Create a script that uses gcloud projects add-iam-policy-binding for all users' email addresses and the Project Viewer role.
    D. Create a new Google Group and add all users to the group. Use gcloud projects add-iam-policy-binding with the Project Viewer role and Group email address.

87. An enterprise migrates to Google Cloud its on-site application. The application uses a license server component. The IP address of the license server is 10.28.0.10. You want the application to be deployed without any code or setup changes. How should the application be implemented?
    A. Create a subnet with a CIDR range of 10.28.0.0/28. Reserve a static internal IP address of 10.28.0.10. Assign the static address to the license server instance.

B. Create a subnet with a CIDR range of 10.28.0.0/10. Reserve a static external IP address of 10.28.0.10. Assign the static address to the license server instance.
C. Create a subnet with a CIDR range of 10.28.0.0/28. Reserve a static external IP address of 10.28.0.10. Assign the static address to the license server instance.
D. Create a subnet with a CIDR range of 10.28.0.0/29. Reserve a static internal IP address of 10.28.0.10. Assign the static address to the license server instance.

88. All thing happens in the API has been fully logged by your developers. The API provides end-users with data requirements such as JSON, XML, CSV, and XLS. It takes a lot of developer effort to support all these formats. Management wants to begin tracking the options used for the following month. What is the quickest way to report on this information at the end of the month without modifying the code?
    A. Export the logs to excel, and search for the different fields.
    B. Create a custom monitoring metric in code and edit the API code to set the metric each time the API is called.
    C. Create a custom counter logging metric that uses a regex to extract the data format into a label. At the end of the month, use the metric viewer to see the group by the label.
    D. Create a log sink that filters for rows that mention the data format. Export that to BigQuery, and run a query at the end of the month.

89. For a few weeks, an organization has been running your marketing application with Autoscaling on the App Engine app, and it has worked well. The marketing team, however, plan a large campaign and expect a great deal of explosive traffic. How do you ensure that 3 idle instances always exist?
    A. Switch to manual scaling and use the idle_instance_count property in the app.yaml.
    B. Set the min_idle_instances property in the app.yaml.
    C. Switch to manual scaling and use the burst_traffic_protection property to True in the app.yaml.
    D. Set the min_instances property in the app.yaml,

90. Your company has appointed external auditors to monitor your system's security. All users and roles configured want to be examined. What is the best way for users and roles to check?

Practice Questions

   A. Ask Auditors to navigate to the IAM page section and check roles and status section
   B. Ask Auditors to navigate to the IAM page and check member and roles section
   C. Ask auditors to check using gclould iam service-accounts list command
   D. Ask auditors to check using gcloud iam roles list command

91. An organization needs to back up data and store for disaster recovery scenarios. They must conduct monthly recovery exercises in accordance with disasters. What is the best standard class for storage?
   A. Coldline
   B. Multi-regional
   C. Nearline
   D. Regional

92. Your project manager wants to delegate to his team members the responsibility for managing cloud storage files and buckets. With the less privileged principle, what role should you play in the team?
   A. Roles/owner
   B. roles/storage.objectCreator
   C. roles/storage.admin
   D. roles/storage.objectAdmin

93. Your application is host in several regions with relational data and static pictures. There are more than 10 TB of data in Your database. For each data type, you want to use a unique storage repository in all areas. For that task, which two products would you choose? (Select any 2)
   A. Cloud Storage
   B. Cloud Spanner
   C. Cloud Bigtable
   D. Cloud SQL

94. A company has a team of developers that are trying to find the best compute service for running a static website. You have a dozen HTML pages, some JavaScript and some CSS files. For the weeks it runs, you need the website highly available. They have a small budget as well. What is the best service for running the site?
   A. Compute engine
   B. Cloud Storage

38

C. Kubernetes Engine
D. App engine

95. A large amount of data stored by BigQuery must be queried by a company. they know that a large amount of data is expected to be returned. What would the cost of the query?
    A. Using Command line, use the --dry_run option on BigQuery to determine the total amount of table data in bytes, as it would be a full scan, and then use the price calculator to determine the cost.
    B. Using Command line, use the --dry_run option on BigQuery to determine the amount of time taken, and then use the price calculator to determine the cost.
    C. Using Command line, use the --dry_run option on BigQuery to determine the number of bytes returned, and then use the price calculator to determine the cost.
    D. Using Command line, use the --dry_run option on BigQuery to determine the number of bytes read, and then use the price calculator to determine the cost.

96. A company has its App Engine application which needs to store stateful data in a proper storage service. The data is non-relational database data. The size of the database is not be expected to grow beyond 10 GB, and they need to have the ability to scale down to zero to avoid unnecessary costs. Which storage service should they use?
    A. Cloud DataStore
    B. Cloud Storage
    C. Cloud Bigtable
    D. Cloud SQL

97. In order to diagnose some errors, your developers try to connect to a Ubuntu server over SSH. The connection times out, however. How you resolve this problem?
    A. gcloud compute firewall-rules create "open-ssh" --network $NETWORK --allow tcp:3389
    B. gcloud compute firewall-rules create "open-ssh" --network $NETWORK --deny tcp:22
    C. gcloud compute firewall-rules create "open-ssh."
    D. gcloud compute firewall-rules create "open-ssh" --network $NETWORK --allow tcp:22

Practice Questions

98. You're working on creating a script that can extract the IP address of a Kubernetes Service. Your coworker sent you a code snippet that they had saved. Which one is the best starting point for your code?
    A. kubectl get svc
    B. kubectl get svc -o html
    C. kubectl get svc -o jsonpath='{.items[*].status.loadBalancer.ingress[0].ip}'
    D. kubectl get svc -o filtered-json='{.items[*].status.loadBalancer.ingress[0].ip}'

99. Your company plans to deploy a Google Cloud web application on a custom Linux distribution. Your website is accessible worldwide and needs to be expanded to satisfy demand. To achieve this objective, select all necessary component from the following: (Select any 2)
    A. Network Load Balancer
    B. Managed Instance Group on Compute Engine
    C. App Engine Standard environment
    D. HTTP Load Balancer

100. A company has to back up data and store all backup data for disaster recovery scenarios. These data would not be available otherwise and would only be required in the event of a disaster. What is the best standard class for storage?
    A. Coldline
    B. Multi-regional
    C. Nearline
    D. Regional

101. A Cloud SQL application is projected to grow dramatically to read uncommonly changing data. How can you boost more read-only customers?
    A. Use backups so you can restore if there's an outage
    B. Configure high availability on the master node
    C. Configure read replicas.
    D. Establish an external replica in the customer's data center

102. Your company asked to add a new IAM member and provide her access to run some queries on BigQuery. Refering to the principle of least privilege, which role should you assign?

A. roles/bigquery.dataOwner and roles/bigquery.jobUser
B. roles/bigquery.dataEditor and roles/bigquery.jobUser
C. roles/bigquery.dataViewer and roles/bigquery.jobUser
D. roles/bigquery.dataViewer and roles/bigquery.user

103. You have a group of managed instances made of preemptive VMs. Every minute all VMs continue to delete and recreate. What might be the reason of this behaviour?
    A. Your managed instance group's health check is repeatedly failing, either to a misconfigured health check or misconfigured firewall rules not allowing the health check to access the instances.
    B. Your managed instance group's VM's are toggled to only last 1 minute in preemptible settings.
    C. Your zonal capacity is limited, causing all preemptible VM's to be shutdown to recover capacity. Try deploying your group to another zone.
    D. You have hit your instance quota for the region.

104. Your financial team works with the engineering team to determine your expenditure on all projects used by your account for each service every day and month. How can data be aggregated and analyzed most easily and flexibly?
    A. Export the data for the billing account(s) involved to a JSON File; use a Cloud Function to listen for a new file in the Storage bucket; code the function to analyze the service data for the desired projects, by day and month.
    B. Use the built-in reports, which already show this data.
    C. Export the data for the billing account(s) involved to BigQuery; then use BigQuery to analyze the service data for the desired projects, by day and month.
    D. Export the data for the billing account(s) to File, import the files into a SQL database; and then use BigQuery to analyze the service data for the desired projects, by day and month.

105. You have been asked by your development team to set up SSL termination load balancer. The website would use the protocol of HTTPS. What should you use to balance the load?
    A. HTTPS Load Balancer
    B. SSL Proxy
    C. HTTP Load Balancer
    D. TCP Proxy

Practice Questions

106. Your company plans to archive data to Cloud Storage that would only be needed in the event of any compliance issues, or Audits. What is the command to create a rare-access storage bucket called ' archive bucket? '
   A. gsutil mb gs://archive_bucket
   B. gsutil rm -coldline gs://archive_bucket
   C. gsutil mb -c coldline gs://archive_bucket
   D. gsutil mb -c nearline gs://archive_bucket

107. You are trying to deploy a new instance using the family of centos 7. You can't remember the family's exact name. Which command can you use to identify the names of the family?
   A. gcloud compute images list
   B. gcloud compute instances list
   C. gcloud compute images show-families
   D. gcloud compute instances show-families

108. You need to help a developer install the extensions of App Engine Go. However, you have forgotten the component's exact name. Which command can you run to display all the options available?
   A. gcloud components list
   B. gcloud config list
   C. gcloud component list
   D. gcloud config components list

109. Your data team works on some new machine learning models. You create multiple output files a day you want to store in a regional bucket. You concentrate on last month's output files. The files must be cleaned up which are older than a month. What is the best way to implement the solution in fewer steps possible?
   A. Create a Cloud Function triggered when objects are added to a bucket. Look at the date on all the files and delete it, if it's older than a month.
   B. Create a Cloud Function triggered when objects are added to a bucket. Look at the date on all the files and move it to Coldline storage if it's older than a month.
   C. Create a lifecycle policy to switch the objects older than a month to Coldline storage.
   D. Create a lifecycle policy to delete the objects older than a month.

Practice Questions

110. For your application that is distributed across a large managed instance group you need a backup / rollback plan. What is the best way to do that?
    A. Have each instance write critical application data to a Cloud Storage bucket.
    B. Use the Rolling Update feature to deploy/roll back versions with different managed instance group templates.
    C. Schedule a cron job to take snapshots of each instance in the group.
    D. Use the managed instance group snapshot function that is included in Compute Engine.

111. In Google App Engine, you need to update an application. The update have risk factors but can only be tested live. What is the best way to implement the risk reduction update?
    A. Deploy the application temporarily and be prepared to pull it back if needed.
    B. Create a new project with the new app version, and then redirect users to the new version.
    C. Warn users that a new app version may have issues and provide a way to contact you if there are problems.
    D. Deploy a new version of the application but use traffic splitting to only direct a small number of users to the new version.

112. Your application has a large international audience and runs stateless virtual machines across multiple locations within a managed group of instances. An application feature allows users to upload and share files with other users. Files should have 30 days availability ; they will then be completely removed from the system. How should you select a storage solution?
    A. A managed instance group of Filestore servers
    B. A Cloud Datastore database
    C. A multi-regional Cloud Storage bucket
    D. Persistent SSD on virtual machine instances

113. Your team uses a monitoring solution from a third party. They asked you to deploy it to all nodes of your cluster of Kubernetes Engine. How can you do this?
    A. Connect to each node via SSH and install the monitoring solution.
    B. Deploy the monitoring pod as a DaemonSet.
    C. Deploy the monitoring pod as a StatefulSet.
    D. Use Deployment Manager to deploy the monitoring solution.

43

Practice Questions

114. A company deploy an application to Compute Engine instance, which should be able to make calls to read from Cloud Storage and Bigtable. You want to make sure that company follow the least privilege principle. How can you check in a simplest way that the code authenticate easily to the required Google Cloud APIs?

    A. Use the default Compute Engine service account and set its scopes. Let the code find the default service account using "Application Default Credentials".

    B. Create a new service account and key with the required limited permissions. Set the instance to use the new service account. Edit the code to use the service account key.

    C. Register the application with the Binary Registration Service and apply the required roles.

    D. Create a new user account with the required roles. Store the credentials in Cloud Key Management Service and download them to the instance in code.

115. Your business plans to migrate to the cloud a number of petabytes of data set. The data set needs 24 hours a day. Your business analysts only have SQL interface experience. Choose the correct option to store data to optimize t for ease of analysis?

    A. Put flat files into Google Cloud Storage.
    B. Load data into Google BigQuery.
    C. Stream data into Google Cloud Datastore.
    D. Insert data into Google Cloud SQL.

116. You created a bucket for storing certain compliance data archives. The data probably would not likely to be viewed. But for at least seven years you have to store it. Select the suitable default storage class?

    A. Regional
    B. Nearline
    C. Multi-regional
    D. Coldline

117. The website crash for several hours due to a recent software update to a static e-commerce site running on Google Cloud. The CTO decides that a back-out / roll-back plan is required for each critical change. Cloud storage is available on the website, and critical changes are frequent. How should the back-out / roll-back plan be implemented?

Practice Questions

A. Create a snapshot of each VM prior to an update, and recover the VM from the snapshot in case of a new version failure.
B. Enable Google Cloud Deployment Manager (CDM) on the project, and define each change with a new CDM template.
C. Enable object versioning on the website's static data files stored in Google Cloud Storage.
D. Create a Nearline copy for the website static data files stored in Google Cloud Storage.

118. A project is using BigQuery. Your task is to list all BigQuery jobs for that project and set this project as the default for the bq command-line tool. What should you do?
    A. Use "gcloud generate config-url" to generate a URL to the Google Cloud Platform Console to set the default project.
    B. Use "bq config set project" to set the default project.
    C. Use "gcloud config set project" to set the default project
    D. Use "bq generate config-url" to generate a URL to the Google Cloud Platform Console to set the default project.

119. Currently you and your team members are working on web application development. you want to deploy to Kubernetes. You currently have a local Dockerfile that works. How can you get the application deployed to Kubernetes?
    A. Use docker to create a container image, push it to the Google Container Registry, deploy the uploaded image to Kubernetes with kubectl.
    B. Use docker to create a container image, push it to the Google Container Registry, deploy the uploaded image to Kubernetes with kubectl.
    C. Use docker to create a container image, save the image to Cloud Storage, deploy the uploaded image to Kubernetes with kubectl.
    D. Use kubectl to push the convert the Dockerfile into a deployment.

120. What is the command to create a storage bucket that is called ' archive bucket ' with access of once a month?
    A. gsutil mb gs://archive_bucket
    B. gsutil rm -coldline gs://archive_bucket
    C. gsutil mb -c coldline gs://archive_bucket
    D. gsutil mb -c nearline gs://archive_bucket

45

Practice Questions

121. Their critical application was hosted by your company on managed instance groups. You want the instances configured without manual interference for resilience and high availability. How should you configured managed instance groups?
    A. Enable auto-healing for the managed instance groups
    B. Enable auto-repairing for the managed instance groups
    C. Enable auto-restarts for the managed instance groups
    D. Enable auto-updating for the managed instance groups

122. You migrate an on-site application to Google Cloud. The application uses a licensing server component. The IP address of this server is 10.28.0.10. You want the application to be deployed without any modification in code or configuration. How should you go about deploying the application?
    A. Create a subnet with a CIDR range of 10.28.0.0/30. Reserve a static internal IP address of 10.28.0.10. Assign the static address to the license server instance.
    B. Create a subnet with a CIDR range of 10.28.0.0/29. Reserve a static internal IP address of 10.28.0.10. Assign the static address to the license server instance.
    C. Create a subnet with a CIDR range of 10.28.0.0/28. Reserve a static internal IP address of 10.28.0.10. Assign the static address to the license server instance.
    D. Create a subnet with a CIDR range of 10.28.0.0/31. Reserve a static internal IP address of 10.28.0.10. Assign the static address to the license server instance.

123. Data have been saved to a cloud storage and to a BigQuery dataset as well. You need to secure your data and provide your Google Cloud platform users with 3 different types of access levels: admin, read / write and read-only. You want to follow recommended practices by Google. What should you do?
    A. At the Project level, add your administrator user accounts to the Owner role, add your read/write user accounts to the Editor role, and add your read-only user accounts to the Viewer role.
    B. Use the appropriate pre-defined IAM roles for each of the access levels needed for Cloud Storage and BigQuery. Add your users to those roles for each of the services.
    C. Create 3 custom IAM roles with appropriate policies for the access levels needed for Cloud Storage and BigQuery. Add your users to the appropriate roles.
    D. At the Organization level, add your administrator user accounts to the Owner role, add your read/write user accounts to the Editor role, and add your read-only user accounts to the Viewer role.

Practice Questions

124. A SysOps administrator has a lifecycle rule set to a multi-regional bucket where versioning of object is enabled. Which statement effect reflects the configuration of the following lifecycle?{ "rule": [{ "action": {"type": "Delete"}, "condition": {"age": 30, "isLive": false} }, { "action": {"type": "SetStorageClass", "storageClass": "COLDLINE"}, "condition": {"age": 365, "matchesStorageClass": "MULTI_REGIONAL"} }] }

   A. Delete objects older than 30 days and move objects to Coldline Storage after 365 days if the storage class in Multi-regional.
   B. Delete archived objects older than 30 days and move objects to Coldline Storage after 365 days if the storage class in Multi-regional.
   C. Move objects to Coldline Storage after 365 days if the storage class in Multi-regional First rule has no effect on the bucket.
   D. Archive objects older than 30 days and move objects to Coldline Storage after 365 days if the storage class in Multi-regional

125. On a windows instance you have installed an SQL server. Your task is to connect to the instance. Select the option with less steps to take to connect with the instance?

   A. Generate Windows user and password. Check security group for 22 firewall rule. Install RDP Client to connect
   B. Generate Windows password. Check security group for 22 firewall rule. Use RDP option from GCP Console to connect
   C. Generate Windows password. Check security group for 3389 firewall rule. Install RDP Client to connect
   D. Generate Windows user and password. Check security group for 3389 firewall rule. Use RDP option from GCP Console to connect

126. A SysOps administrator has a lifecycle rule set to a multi-regional bucket where versioning of object is enabled. Which statement effect reflects the configuration of the following lifecycle? { "rule": [{ "action": {"type": "Delete"}, "condition": {"age": 30, "isLive": false} }, { "action": {"type": "SetStorageClass", "storageClass": "COLDLINE"}, "condition": {"age": 365, "matchesStorageClass": "MULTI_REGIONAL"} }] }

   A. Move objects to Coldline Storage after 365 days if the storage class in Multi-regional First rule has no effect on the bucket.
   B. Delete archived objects older than 30 days and move objects to Coldline Storage after 365 days if the storage class in Multi-regional.
   C. Delete objects older than 30 days and move objects to Coldline Storage after 365 days if the storage class in Multi-regional.

D. Archive objects older than 30 days and move objects to Coldline Storage after 365 days if the storage class in Multi-regional

127. Your company assigns you the task to take streaming data from thousands of Internet of Things (IoT) devices, ingest it, run it through a processing pipeline, and finally store it for analysis. For data analysis you have to run SQL queries. Choos e the correct option you would use for this task?
   A. App Engine, Cloud Dataflow, BigQuery
   B. Cloud Pub/Sub, Cloud Dataflow, BigQuery
   C. Cloud Pub/Sub, Cloud Dataflow, Cloud Dataproc
   D. Cloud Dataflow, Cloud Pub/Sub, BigQuery

128. Your company has deployed its application to managed groups of instances that are served by a network load balancer. They want health checks enabled for these instances. How could you achieve this?
   A. Perform the health check using HTTPS by hosting a basic web server
   B. Perform the health check using HTTP by hosting a basic web server
   C. Perform the health check using TCP
   D. Update Managed Instance groups to send a periodic ping to the network load balancer

129. You want to create a new Kubernetes Cluster on Google Cloud Platform. You want to configure the nodes without any manual intervention for resilience and high availability. how should you configure this cluster?
   A. Enable auto-repairing for the nodes
   B. Enable auto-healing for the nodes
   C. Enable auto-upgrades for the nodes
   D. Enable auto-healing for the managed instance groups

130. The monthly budget for your project is reserved by your company. If you are approaching the limit, you want to be informed automatically about your project expenditure. What are you supposed to do?
   A. In App Engine Settings, set a daily budget at the rate of 1/30 of your monthly budget.
   B. In the GCP Console, configure billing export to BigQuery. Create a saved view that queries your total spend.
   C. Link a credit card with a monthly limit equal to your budget.

Practice Questions

D. Create a budget alert for desired percentages such as 50%, 90%, and 100% of your total monthly budget.

131. You were asked to add a new IAM member and give them access to BigQuery for running queries. Referring to the best practices and the principle of least privilege recommended by Google, how would you assign them access?

A. Assign roles/bigquery.dataViewer and roles/bigquery.jobUser roles to a group; add users to groups

B. Assign roles/bigquery.dataViewer and roles/bigquery.jobUser roles to the users

C. Create a custom role with roles/bigquery.dataViewer and roles/bigquery.jobUser roles; assign custom role to the group; add users to groups

D. Create a custom role with roles/bigquery.dataViewer and roles/bigquery.jobUser roles; assign custom role to the users

132. You provide suggestion to your company that move the infrequently accessed data to the cloud for cost reduction. To refresh historical charts, still data will be accessed approximately once a month. Furthermore, data over 5 years of age must be archived for 5 years for reasons of compliance. How should the data be stored and managed?

A. In Google Cloud Storage and stored in a Multi-Regional bucket. Set an Object Lifecycle Management policy to change the storage class to Coldline for data older than 5 years.

B. In Google Cloud Storage and stored in a Nearline bucket. Set an Object Lifecycle Management policy to delete data older than 5 years.

C. In Google Cloud Storage and stored in a Nearline bucket. Set an Object Lifecycle Management policy to change the storage class to Coldline for data older than 5 years.

D. In Google Cloud Storage and stored in a Multi-Regional bucket. Set an Object Lifecycle Management policy to delete data older than 5 years.

133. You created a Kubernetes deployment with 3 replicas on your cluster, called Deployment-A. Deployment-B requires access to Deployment-A. Deployment-A can't be exposed outside the cluster. What are you going to do?

A. Create a Service of type LoadBalancer for Deployment A and an Ingress Resource for that Service. Have Deployment B use the Ingress IP address.

B. Create a Service of type NodePort for Deployment A and an Ingress Resource for that Service. Have Deployment B use the Ingress IP address.

C. Create a Service of type LoadBalancer for Deployment A. Have Deployment B use the Service IP address.

D. Create a Service of type ClusterIP for Deployment A. Have Deployment B use the Service IP address.

134. Your company wants to track whether someone is present for a scheduled meeting in a meeting room. There are 1000 meeting rooms in 5 offices in 3 continents. Each room has a motion sensor that provide status of every second. The motion sensor data only includes a sensor identity and various separate data items for information. This data and information about account owners and office locations will be used by analysts. What kind of database do you want to use?

A. NoSQL
B. Relational
C. Blobstore
D. Flat file

135. You tried to deploy a container to Kubernetes, but it seems that Kubectl can not connect to the cluster. What is the most probable reason for this and how can you correct it?

A. The firewall rules are preventing the connection. Open up the firewall rules to allow traffic to port 1337.
B. The kubeconfig is missing the credentials. Run the gcloud container clusters auth login command.
C. The kubeconfig is missing the credentials. Run the gcloud container clusters get-credentials command.
D. The firewall rules are preventing the connection. Open up the firewall rules to allow traffic to port 3682.

136. The Compute engine instances are used by your company for multiple applications. You want to make instances resilient to crashes or termination of the system. How are the instances to be configured?

A. Set onHostMaintenance availability policy to terminate instances
B. Set onHostMaintenance availability policy to migrate instances
C. Set automaticRestart availability policy to false
D. Set automaticRestart availability policy to true

Practice Questions

137. A company want to enable running Google Container Engine cluster to scale as demand for the application changes. What should they do?
    A. Update the existing Container Engine cluster with the following command: gcloud alpha container clusters update mycluster --enable-autoscaling --min-nodes=1 --max-nodes=10
    B. Create a new Container Engine cluster with the following command:gcloud alpha container clusters create mycluster --enable-autoscaling --min-nodes=1 --max-nodes=10and redeploy your application
    C. Add a tag to the instances in the cluster with the following command:gcloud compute instances add-tags INSTANCE --tags --enable-autoscaling max-nodes-10
    D. Add additional nodes to your Container Engine cluster using the following command: gcloud container clusters resize CLUSTER_Name --size 10

138. For the further analysis of possible legal proceedings, your organization requires that metrics for all applications be retained for 5 years. Which approach they should use?
    A. Grant the security team access to the logs in each Project
    B. Configure Stackdriver Monitoring for all Projects, and export to BigQuery
    C. Configure Stackdriver Monitoring for all Projects, and export to Google Cloud Storage
    D. Configure Stackdriver Monitoring for all Projects with the default retention policies

139. You have created the code for Cloud Function to respond to HTTP triggers and return certain data in JSON format. The code is locally available ; it is tested and working. How do you use the command in Google Cloud to create the function?
    A. gcloud function create
    B. gcloud functions deploy
    C. gcloud function deploy
    D. gcloud functions create

140. You have been asked by your security team to present certain numbers based on the logs exported to BigQuery. Your manager requested you to determine what the query costs due to the team structure. Choose the best option to calculate the cost?
    A. Create the query and execute the query in "cost estimation mode"
    B. It's not possible to estimate the cost of a query.

C. Create the query and use the --dry_run option to determine the amount of data read, and then use the price calculator to determine the cost.
   D. Use the BigQuery index viewer to determine how many records you'll be reading.

141. An organization created a Kubernetes engine cluster called ' Project-1 '. They realized that the cluster must be modified from n1-standard-1 to n1-standard-4. What is the command for this modification?
    A. gcloud container clusters update project-1 --machine-type n1-standard-4
    B. gcloud container clusters resize project-1 --machine-type n1-standard-4
    C. Create a new node pool in the same cluster, and migrate the workload to the new pool.
    D. gcloud container clusters migrate project-1 --machine-type n1-standard-4

142. You write a Python script for Google Compute Engine virtual machine to connect to Google BigQuery. The script is printing connection errors to BigQuery. How would you fix the script issue?
    A. Run your script on a new virtual machine with the BigQuery access scope enabled
    B. Create a new service account with BigQuery access and execute your script with that user
    C. Install the bq component for gcloud with the command gcloud components install bq.
    D. Install the latest BigQuery API client library for Python

143. Your task is to obtain only the public SSH keys of the operations team onto a specific Bastion host instance of a particular project. Currently, all instances within the projects have already been granted wide project access. How do you block or override the project level access on the Bastion host in few steps?
    A. Use the gcloud compute project-info add-metadata [INSTANCE_NAME] --metadata block-project-ssh-keys=FALSE command to block the access.
    B. Project wide SSH access cannot be overridden or blocked and needs to be removed.
    C. Use the gcloud compute instances add-metadata [INSTANCE_NAME] --metadata block-project-ssh-keys=TRUE command to block the access
    D. Use the gcloud compute instances add-metadata [INSTANCE_NAME] --metadata block-project-ssh-keys=FALSE command to block the access.

Practice Questions

144. For your colleagues, you want to assign a new role applied to all the current and future organization projects. BigQuery Job User and Cloud Bigtable user roles should be included in this role. You want to follow Google's recommended practices. How should you create the required new role?
    A. For your organization, in the Google Cloud Platform Console under Roles, select both roles and combine them into a new custom role.
    B. For all projects, in the Google Cloud Platform Console under Roles, select both roles and combine them into a new custom role.
    C. For one of your projects, in the Google Cloud Platform Console under Roles, select both roles and combine them into a new custom role. Use gcloud iam promote-role to promote the role from a project role to an organization role.
    D. Use gcloud iam combine-roles --global to combine the 2 roles into a new custom role.

145. In the development environment, you created an App engine application. The tests were successful for the application. It is required to move the application to production environment. How can the application be deployed in minimum steps?
    A. Clone the app engine application to the production environment
    B. Perform app engine deploy using the --project parameter
    C. Activate the production config, perform app engine deploy
    D. Change the project parameter in app.yaml and redeploy

146. There is a cluster of Kubernetes with 1 node-pool. The cluster receives heavy traffic and needs to be expanded. You plan to add an additional node. What are you supposed to do?
    A. Edit the managed instance group of the cluster and enable autoscaling.
    B. Edit the managed instance group of the cluster and increase the number of VMs by 1.
    C. Use "kubectl container clusters resize" with the desired number of nodes.
    D. Use "gcloud container clusters resize" with the desired number of nodes.

147. Looking at your private Github repo source code for your application, you noticed that service account key has been committed to a git. What steps should you take next?
    A. Contact Google Cloud Support

B. Revoke the key, remove the key from Git, purge the Git history to remove all traces of the file, ensure the key is added to the .gitignore file.
C. Do nothing. Git is fine for keys if the repo is private.
D. Delete the project and create a new one.

148. Your industry wants to try cloud with low-risk factor. They want to archive about 100 TB of their log data into the cloud and test the analytics features they can find there, while retaining that data as a backup for long-term disaster recovery. Which two steps should they take? (Choose two answers)
    A. Load logs into Google BigQuery.
    B. Upload log files into Google Cloud Storage.
    C. Insert logs into Google Cloud Bigtable.
    D. Import logs into Google Stackdriver.
    E. Load logs into Google Cloud SQL.

149. A user would like to install a Cloud Shell tool. The tool should be available throughout the sessions. Where should this tool be installed by the user?
    A. /bin
    B. /usr/local/bin
    C. /google/scripts
    D. ~/bin

150. A company wishes to use the Deployment Manager to deploy its application. However, it would like to understand how changes will affect the update before it is implemented. How can the company achieve this?
    A. Use Deployment Manager Dry Run feature
    B. Use Deployment Manager Validate Deployment feature
    C. Use Deployment Manager Preview feature
    D. Use Deployment Manager Snapshot feature

151. Workers created a deployment for an application container. The deployment can be checked under Workloads in the Console. The workers are out for the rest for a week, and you need to complete the setup by exposing the workload. What is the easiest way to perform this?
    A. Create a new Service that points to the existing deployment
    B. Create a new Daemon Set

C. Create a Global Load Balancer that points to the pod in the deployment.
D. Create a Static IP Address Resource for the Deployment.

152. You are trying to deploy a new instance which uses the centos seven family. You cannot recall the exact name of the family. Which command is used to determine the family name?
    A. gcloud compute instances list
    B. gcloud compute images show-families
    C. gcloud compute instances show-families
    D. gcloud compute images list

153. What is the efficient way to make sure that the nodes in the Kubernetes cluster are always up-to-date with the latest stable version of the Kubernetes?
    A. Opt into the Kubernetes Node Update program from the quotas page
    B. Run the kubectl nodes update command
    C. Run the kubectl nodes upgrade command
    D. Enable the automatic node upgrades setting

154. An auto-scaled managed instance group is set to scale based on the CPU utilization of 60%. There are currently three instances present in the instance group. You are connected with one of the instance and check that the CPU utilization is up to 70%. But the instance group is not starting up another instance. What would be the reason?
    A. The autoscaler is disabled
    B. The autoscaler takes 60 seconds before creating a new instance
    C. The load balancer does not recognize the instance as healthy
    D. The average CPU for the entire instance group is below 60%

155. A company has hired a third-party analytics company to help find patterns in user data. The development team has generated a file which contains only the data that have requested, which contains personally identifiable information. What is the easiest way to share the data with another company?
    A. Create a new user for the company and grant them access to the original data source for them to query
    B. Send the file through email

C. Put the data on Cloud Storage and generate a signed URL that will expire in one hour, and securely share the URL

D. Put the data on Cloud Storage in a public bucket and securely share the URL

156. Developers are trying to select the Compute service to run a static website. They have a dozen HTML pages, few Javascript, and some CSS. They want that the site must be highly available for the few weeks it is running, but they have a limited budget. Which service is used to run the site?

A. Kubernetes Engine
B. Compute Engine
C. Cloud Storage
D. App Engine

157. A team is using a third party monitoring solution. They want you to deploy it to all nodes in a Kubernetes Engine Cluster. What is the possible way to do it?

A. Connect to each node via SSH and install the monitoring solution
B. Deploy the monitoring pod as a Deployment
C. Deploy the monitoring pod as a DaemonSet
D. Use the Deployment Manager to deploy the monitoring solution

158. A development team requires a regional MySQL database with point-in-time recovery for a new proof-of-concept application. What is the possible way to enable point-in-time recovery?

A. Replicate to a Cloud Spanner database
B. Create a read replica in the same region
C. Enable binary logging
D. Create hourly back-ups

159. An App Engine application is working as front-end and going to publish messages to Pub/Sub. The public API has not been enabled yet. What is the best way to enable the API?

A. Use a service account to auto-enable the API.
B. Enable the API in the Console
C. Application's in App Engine do not require external APIs to be enabled
D. The API will be enabled the first time the code attempts to access Pub/Sub

Practice Questions

160. You want to deploy a simple web application securely and inexpensively. The application is running within the Docker at port 8080. Once the deployment is completed, the developer is going to take ownership of the deployment. What is a suitable environment for running the application?
    A. Use an App Engine Standard Environment
    B. Use an App Engine Flexible Environment
    C. Use an on-premises Kubernetes cluster
    D. Use Kubernetes Engine

161. A network team wants to audit the network traffic inside the network. How can you make sure that they have access to data which they require?
    A. Enable Flow Logs.
    B. Disable Flow Logs.
    C. Add them to the subnet traffic viewer role.
    D. Add a firewall capture filter.

162. Some PDFs are uploaded to a public bucket. When the user browses to the document, they have downloaded it rather than browsing it. How can you make sure that the PDFs are viewed in the browser?
    A. This is a browser setting and not something that can be changed
    B. Use the gsutil set file-type pdf command
    C. Set the Content metadata for the object to "application/pdf."
    D. Set the Content-Type metadata for the object to "application/pdf."

163. You are trying to deploy a container to Kubernetes, but kubectl does not seem to be capable of connecting to the cluster. How can you fix this issue?
    A. The kubeconfig is missing the credentials. Run the gcloud container clusters get-credentials command
    B. The firewall rules are preventing the connection. Open up the firewall rules to allow traffic to port 1337
    C. The kubeconfig is missing the credentials. Run the gcloud container clusters auth login command
    D. The firewall rules are preventing the connection. Open up the firewall rules to allow traffic to port 3682

Practice Questions

164. A Deployment Manager is used to deploy the application to an auto-scaled, managed, instance group of Compute Engine. The application is a single binary. What is the efficient way to get the binary onto the instance, without any complexity?
    A. When creating the instance template use the startup script metadata key to bootstrap the application
    B. Use a "golden image" that contains everything you need
    C. When creating the instance template, use the startup script metadata key to install Ansible. Have the instance run the play-book at startup to install the application
    D. Once the instance starts up, connect over SSH and install the application

165. A Linux server is running on a custom network. There is an allow firewall rule having an IP filter of 0.0.0.0/0 with the port of TCP 22. The logs on the instance represent a continuous stream of attempts from different IP addresses trying to connect via SSH. You suspect that this is a brute force attack. How can you change the firewall rule to stop this and still enable access for legit users?
    A. Stop the instance.
    B. Deny all traffic to port 22
    C. Change the port that SSH is running on in the instance and change the port number in the firewall rule
    D. Change the IP address range in the filter to only allow known IP addresses

166. Pub/ Sub-topic is used to publish the disparate messages from on-premise applications. You are looking for a simple way to run some code, every time before publishing the message. What is the best solution which is cost effective and requires less CPU utilization?
    A. Use a scheduled task that starts an App Engine application to poll for changes
    B. Use a scheduled Cloud Function to check the queue every minute
    C. Deploy code to Compute Engine that polls for messages
    D. Have Pub/Sub push messages to a Cloud Function

167. A team is working using desired state configuration for the entire infrastructure, that's why they are excited to store the Kuernetes Deployment in YAML. You have created a Kubernetes deployment with the kubectl apply command and passed this on a YAML file. You need to edit the number of replicas. How can you update the deployment?
    A. Edit the number of replicas in the YAML file and rerun the kubectl apply

B. Edit the YAML and push it to Github so that the git triggers deploy the change.
C. Disregard the YAML file. Use the kubectl scale command
D. Edit the number of replicas in the YAML file and run the kubectl set image command

168. A team is building a web application. The plan is to deploy Kubernetes. A Docker file is working locally. How can you get the application deployed to Kubernetes?
    A. Use kubectl to push the convert the Dockerfile into a deployment
    B. Use docker to create a container image, save the image to Cloud Storage, deploy the uploaded image to Kubernetes with kubectl
    C. Use kubectl apply to push the Dockerfile to Kubernetes
    D. Use docker to create a container image, push it to the Google Container Registry, deploy the uploaded image to Kubernetes with kubectl

169. A developer has created an application which is required to make calls to Cloud Storage and BigQuery. The code will run inside the container and will run on Kubernetes Engine and on-premise. What is the easiest way for them to authenticate to the services of Google Cloud?
    A. Create a service account, grant it the least visible privileges to the required services, generate and download a key. Use the key to authenticate inside the application
    B. Use the default service account for App Engine which already has the required permissions
    C. Use the default service account for Compute Engine which already has the required permissions
    D. Create a service account, with editor permissions, generate and download a key. Use the key to authenticate inside the application

170. It is required to create a new development Kubernetes cluster with four nodes. The cluster will be named as "Linux-academy-dev-cluster." How will this cluster be created?
    A. gcloud container clusters create Linux-academy-dev-cluster --num-nodes 4
    B. kubectl clusters create Linux-academy-dev-cluster 4
    C. kubectl clusters create Linux-academy-dev-cluster --num-nodes 4
    D. gcloud container clusters create Linux-academy-dev-cluster 4

Practice Questions

171. A new firewall rule is created to allow incoming traffic on port 22, by using a target tag named as "dev-ssh." When you tried to connect to one of your instances, you are unable to do so. How can you resolve this problem?
    A. Run the gcloud firewall-rules refresh command
    B. Use source tags in place of the target tags
    C. Reboot the instances for the firewall rule to take effect
    D. Apply a network tag of "dev-ssh" to the instance you're trying to connect into and test again

172. A developer is logging everything that happened in the API and API allows the end users to request the data in the form of JSON, XML, CSV, XLS. A lot of developers effort is required for supporting all of these formats. And management starts tracking which of the option will be used over the next month. Without making any changes to the code, what is the best possible way to report this data at the end of the month?
    A. Create a custom counter logging metric that uses a regex to extract the data format into a label. At the end of the month, use the metric viewer to see the group by the label
    B. Create a log sink that filters for rows that mention the data format. Export that to BigQuery, and run a query at the end of the month
    C. Create a custom monitoring metric in code and edit the API code to set the metric each time the API is called
    D. Export the logs to excel, and search for the different fields

173. You want to connect to one of your Compute Engine instances by using SSH. You do not have an SSH key deployed yet, but you have authenticated gcloud. How can you connect to the app easily?
    A. Create a key with the ssh-keygen command. Upload the key to the instance. Run gcloud compute instances list to get the IP address of the instance, then use the ssh command
    B. Use the gcloud compute ssh command
    C. Create a key with the ssh-keygen command. Then use the gcloud compute ssh command
    D. Run gcloud compute instances list to get the IP address of the instance, then use the ssh command

Practice Questions

174. You have created a sink which exports all of your project logs to Cloud Storage. But there are new records seen in the log viewer. However, they are not present in the storage bucket. What could be the reason?
    A. Cloud Storage isn't a supported destination
    B. Each log sink destination has its time window for saving the data
    C. The Cloud Storage Bucket doesn't have the correct permissions
    D. You forgot to enable the sink inside the Cloud Storage UI

175. Before creating an instance with a GPU, what must you do? (Choose 2)
    A. You must make sure that the appropriate GPU driver is installed
    B. You must select which boot disk image you want to use for the instance
    C. Nothing. GPU drivers are automatically included with the boot disk images
    D. You must only select the GPU driver type. The correct base image is selected automatically

176. Through which command you can view the properties of active configuration in SDK?
    A. gcloud config list
    B. gcloud auth login
    C. gcloud auth list
    D. gcloud debug

177. Company developer keeps trying to execute a command, and he suspects something is wrong while there is no mistake. Now he wants to check the gcloud logs in order to manage the stack driver logging then which command is used for this purpose?
    A. gcloud
    B. gcloud logging
    C. gcloud info
    D. google logs

178. An enterprise is attempting to build on the Cloud SDK; a new compute instance using the creation command of the compute group and the subgroup of instances. Some flags they forgot and want to look up with the man pages. How will do this?
    A. man compute_instances_create

B. man gcloud compute instances create
C. man gcloud-compute-instances-create
D. man gcloud_compute_instances_create

179. A user try to run the following command on his computer, "$ gcloud alpha cloud-shell scp –help " and it gives an error "Invalid choice 'alpha." What was the reason behind this?
    A. The alpha component isn't installed.
    B. The project property is set to the wrong project.
    C. The user account doesn't have permission to execute alpha commands.
    D. The cloud-shell command was moved from alpha to beta.

180. To set up a File-based billing export which component you can use?
    A. A Budget and at least one alert.
    B. A BigQuery dataset.
    C. A Cloud Storage bucket.
    D. A Bigtable

181. A company CEO said to the accounting department to keep track of expenditure on a specific account. He also said that he prefers to use Excel to create the reports in order to avoid learning new tools. What would be the best export option?
    A. Download the monthly XLS report
    B. SQL Export
    C. File Export with CSV
    D. File Export with JSON

182. An official budget alert review process is in place for your finance team. They have their own data tracking software. The software has a REST API for submitting information. You have requested that your software be automatedly integrated with Google Cloud alerts. How do you do?
    A. Use a bot to listen for emails from Google Cloud regarding notifications
    B. Use Pub/Sub notifications and listen for messages with a Cloud Function.
    C. Export to Cloud Storage with the File export, and process the files with a daily scheduled task.
    D. Export to BigQuery and perform daily analysis.

Practice Questions

183. Your development team requested your assistance. You have to need to create and terminate a new compute engine instance in a simple, reproducible manner so that you can automate it as part of your CI / CD process. What is the best way to achieve this?
    A. Show them how to use a Docker container. Then they can get rid of the need for the VM.
    B. Show them how to use the Console to create and terminate instances.
    C. Recommend that they use the REST API to develop the functionality in the language of their choosing.
    D. Show them how to use the gcloud component of the Cloud SDK.

184. You were hired to a two-year-old start-up company as a cloud engineer. They recently had a little downsizing, and several engineers left the company to pursue various projects. It appears that a core project seems to have been deleted shortly after one of them leaves. What is the most probable reason for deleting the project?
    A. A failed attempt to pay the bill resulted in Google deleting the project.
    B. The project was created by one of the engineers and not attached to the organization.
    C. One of the engineers intentionally deleted the project out of spite.
    D. You've been the victim of the latest malware that deletes one project per hour until you pay them to stop.

185. You need to help a developer to install the App Engine Go extension. However, you forgot the component's exact name. What command could you execute to display all available options?
    A. gcloud components list
    B. gcloud config components list
    C. gcloud component list
    D. gcloud config list

186. A company has been asked to its developer to add a new IAM member and grant them access to run some queries on BigQuery. Considering the principle of least privilege, which role should developer assign?
    A. roles/bigquery.dataOwner
    B. roles/bigquery.admin

C. Project Editor
D. roles/bigquery.dataViewer and roles/bigquery.jobUser

187. As for the audit logs, the best practice recommended by Google is which of the following?
    A. Export your audit logs to Cloud Storage and store them for a long period of time.
    B. Flush your audit logs monthly so you can more easily notice security events.
    C. Export your audit logs to Pub/Sub.
    D. Export your audit logs to App Engine.

188. An enterprise security team was unwilling to move to the cloud as they don't have the visibility of the network they are used to. What could help them learn about your Google Cloud network as an attractive feature?
    A. Firewall rules
    B. Flow logs
    C. Subnets
    D. Routes

189. How you add a new user who is hired as a new employee and give them access to its team's project.
    A. Add the user inside of G Suite; sync from G Suite to the Active Directory using the Directory Sync util; add them as a member and grant them the required roles.
    B. Add them as a member of the project, grant them the required roles, and sync the user back to G Suite.
    C. Add the user inside of G Suite, create a user group inside of GCP IAM settings, and add them to that user group.
    D. Add the user inside of G Suite, add them as a member of the project, and grant them the required roles.

190. From the following option which is the use case of Flow Logs?
    A. Serving as a UDP relay.
    B. Proxying SSL traffic.
    C. Network forensics.
    D. Blocking instances from communicating over certain ports.

191. The company deploys an application, and it will require calls for read from Cloud Storage and Bigtable. They want to ensure that follow the least privilege principle. The only instance in this project is this Compute Engine instance. How can the code authenticate easily to the Google Cloud APIs needed?
    A. Register the application with the Binary Registration Service and apply for the required roles.
    B. Create a new user account with the required roles. Store the credentials in Cloud Key Management Service and download them to the instance in code.
    C. Create a new service account and key with the required limited permissions. Set the instance to use the new service account. Edit the code to use the service account key.
    D. Use the default Compute Engine service account and set its scopes. Let the code find the default service account using "Application Default Credentials."

192. You have 3 buckets for cloud storage, which store all sensitive data. To make sure these buckets are not public, which guarantee that?
    A. allUsers and allAuthenticatedUsers
    B. allAuthenticatedUsers
    C. allpublicUsers
    D. allUsers

193. In your development project, you have configured and tested several personalized roles. How quickly is your new production project to create the same roles?
    A. Use the gcloud iam roles copy command and set the destination project.
    B. In the UI, select the roles and click the Export button.
    C. Use the gcloud iam copy roles command and set the destination project.
    D. Recreate them in the new project.

194. A new member of the big-data team was asked to help you on board. He needs full BigQuery access. What type of role would be most efficient to play in compliance with the less privileged principle?
    A. Managed Role
    B. Primitive Role
    C. Predefined Role
    D. Custom Role

Practice Questions

195. An organization plans to migrate to Google Cloud from an on-site application. The application uses a licensing server component. The IP address is 10.28.0.10 on the license server. They want the app to be deployed without any code or setup changes. How should the application be deployed?
    A. Create a subnet with a CIDR range of 10.28.0.0/29. Reserve a static internal IP address of 10.28.0.10. Assign the static address to the license server instance.
    B. Create a subnet with a CIDR range of 10.28.0.0/28. Reserve a static internal IP address of 10.28.0.10. Assign the static address to the license server instance.
    C. Create a subnet with a CIDR range of 10.28.0.0/28. Reserve a static external IP address of 10.28.0.10. Assign the static address to the license server instance.
    D. Create a subnet with a CIDR range of 10.28.0.0/10. Reserve a static external IP address of 10.28.0.10. Assign the static address to the license server instance.

196. You've run your app with Autoscaling for a couple of weeks, and it worked well. Your marketing team, however, plans a massive campaign and expects a great deal of explosive traffic. How do you ensure that four idle instances are always present?
    A. Switch to manual scaling and use the idle_instance_count property in the app.yaml.
    B. Switch to manual scaling and use the burst_traffic_protection property to True in the app.yaml.
    C. Set the min_instances property in the app.yaml,
    D. Set the min_idle_instances property in the app.yaml

197. An n-tier application with an Apache web server is running on Compute Engine that serves web requests. All your logging into Stackdriver should be consolidated. What is the best approach to stack driver with Apache logs?
    A. Install the Stackdriver monitoring and logging agents on the instance
    B. Enable Stackdriver monitoring when creating the instance.
    C. Stackdriver logs application data from all instances by default.
    D. Create a log sink and export it to Stackdriver.

198. You have to get all public SSH keys of your team on all instances of a specific project. You gathered all of them. What is the simplest way to deploy your keys with the fewest possible steps?
    A. Format all of the keys as needed and then, using the user interface, upload each key one at a time.

B. Use the gcloud compute ssh command to upload all the keys
C. Add all of the keys into a file that's formatted according to the requirements. Use the "gcloud compute project-info add-metadata" command to upload the keys.
D. Add all of the keys into a file that's formatted according to the requirements. Use the "gcloud compute instances add-metadata" command to upload the keys to each instance

199. You are trying to provide some files in a cloud storage bucket with temporary access. You would like to limit the availability of the files to 30 minutes. How you generate a signed URL in a few steps as possible?
    A. Create a service account and JSON key. Use the "gsutil signurl -d 30m " command and pass in the JSON key and bucket.
    B. In the UI select the objects and click the "Sign With Key" button.
    C. Create a service account and JSON key. Use the "gsutil signurl -t 10m" command and pass in the JSON key and bucket.
    D. In the UI select the objects and click the Generate Signed URL button

200. GCP documentation states that you can set a budget to help you in:
    A. Project Planning.
    B. Cost Optimization.
    C. Both of the Above.
    D. None of the Above.

201. The purpose behind creating a budget is so that you can trigger alert notifications which are sent to the:
    A. Billing Administrators.
    B. Billing Account Users.
    C. Both A and B.
    D. None of the Above.

202. With how many components, Data Flow is fundamentally associated?
    A. Three Components.
    B. Two Components.
    C. Four Components.

Practice Questions

    D. Five Components.

203. Moving data could also mean:
 A. Loading some data from disk into memory.
 B. Loading some data from memory into the disk.
 C. Both A and B.
 D. None of the Above.

204. A _____ is the simplified version of reality, which is used by your mind to anticipate events or conclude them.
 A. Data Flow.
 B. Mental Model.
 C. Cloud Shell Data Flow.
 D. None of the Above.

205. Data Flow consists of?
 A. Compute Service.
 B. Storage Service.
 C. Network Service.
 D. All of the Above.

206. _____ is a platform of cloud computing services that grew with the Google App Engine framework which is used for hosting web applications from Google's data centers.
 A. GCP.
 B. AWS.
 C. Azure.
 D. None of the Above

207. Compute Engine in Compute Products can be described as:
 A. Virtual Machines.
 B. Disks.
 C. Networks.
 D. All of the Above.

208. Each GCP project contains:
    A. A project name.
    B. A project ID.
    C. A project number.
    D. All of the Above.

209. Cloud Function is described as Event-driven server less function. Cloud Function even performs faster than the Compute Engine within the 10th of the second and manages all the scaling for you automatically.
    A. Event-driven server less function.
    B. Event-driven function.
    C. Serverless function.
    D. None of the Above.

210. The Cloud TPU is enlisted in:
    A. Compute Products Section.
    B. Storage Product Section.
    C. AI and Machine Learning Section.
    D. Data and Analytics Section.

211. Your billing data can be accessed by using:
    A. BigQuery.
    B. Big Analytics.
    C. Analytics.
    D. None of the Above.

212. Setting a budget lets you track your cost of growth towards that amount.
    A. True.
    B. False.

213. Google automatically creates a project for your:
    A. Administrator Account.

B. User Account.
C. Administrator and User Account.
D. Does not create any project

Answers

1. **A** (Turn on Stackdriver Logging during the Kubernetes Engine cluster creation.)

   E (Use the Stackdriver Logging export feature to create a sink to BigQuery. Specify a filter expression to export log records related to your Kubernetes Engine cluster only.)

   Explanation:
   Creation of cluster using Stackdriver logging will enable the container logs to be stored in Stackdriver logging. Stackdriver logging also supports exporting of logs to BigQuery by creating sinks.

2. **D** (The desired GPU doesn't exist in that zone.)

   Explanation:
   GPU availability varies in between region to region and zone to zone. One GPU available in one region/zone is not the guarantee to be available in another region/zone.

3. **C** (Install with Cloud Launcher Marketplace.)

   Explanation:
   Cloud Launcher provides deployments which are completely transparent to you, and it takes no time in completion.

4. **B** (Create a sink to BigQuery and provide BigQuery access to the billing department.)

   Explanation:
   Billing data can be automatically exported to BigQuery. BigQuery provides the SQL interface for the billing department to query the data.

5. **D** (Pub/Sub, Bigtable.)

   Explanation:
   Pub/Sub is ideal for data ingestion, and Bigtable is used for data storage in time series.

6. **C** (Configure Stackdriver Monitoring for all Projects, and export to Google Cloud Storage.)

   Explanation:

Answers

Stackdriver monitoring metrics can be exported to Google Cloud Storage or BigQuery. When the logs need to be archived, GCS is a better option.

7. **C** (Set onHostMaintenance availability policy to migrate instances.)

Explanation:

onHostMaintenance availability policy determines how the instances react on the host maintenance events.

8. **D** (Create a new project in the asia-east2 region and create an app engine in the project.)

Explanation:

App Engine is a regional resource, and it needs to be redeployed to multiple different regions.

9. **A** (Generate a signed URL to the Stackdriver export destination for auditors to access.)
   C (Export audit logs to Cloud Storage via an export sink.)

Explanation:

Stackdriver logging allows export to Cloud Storage which can be used for long term access and exposed to external auditors using signed URLs.

10. **C** (roles/storage.objectCreator.)

Explanation:

Roles/storage.objectCreator allows the users to create objects. It does not permit to view, delete, or overwrite the objects.

11. **D** (File Export with CSV.)

Explanation:

Cloud Billing allows export of the billing data as flat files in CSV and JSON format. As the billing department wants to use Excel to create their reports, CSV would be an ideal option.

12. **D** (gsutil iam ch allUsers:objectViewer gs://bucket-name)

Explanation:

Answers

The bucket can be shared by providing the Storage Object Viewer access to all Users.

13. **C** (Create a managed instance group based on the instance template. Configure autoscaling based on HTTP traffic and configure the instance group as the backend service of an HTTP load balancer.)

Explanation:
The instance template can be used with the managed instance group to define autoscaling to scale as per demand, which can then be exposed through a load balancer as a backend service.

14. **B** (Configure a single VPC with two subnets having the different CIDR range hosted in the different region.)

Explanation:
VMs need to be able to communicate using private IPs they should be hosted in the same VPC. The Subnets can be in any region; however, they should have a non-overlapping CIDR range.

15. **C** (Use Live migration to move to machine type with higher memory.)

Explanation:
Live migration would help migrate the instance to a machine-type with higher memory with minimal to no downtime.

16. **C** (Store the file in Cloud Storage. Generate a signed URL with 4 hours expiry and share it with the auditors.)

Explanation:
The file can be stored in Cloud Storage, and Signed URLs can be used to quickly and securely share the files with the third party.

17. **B** (Add the finance team members to the Billing Administrator role for each of the billing accounts that they need to manage. Add the developers to the Viewer role for the Project.)

Explanation:

Answers

As there are two requirements, Finance team able to set budgets on the project but not view project contents and developers able to only view billing charges of their projects. Finance with Billing Administrator role can set budgets and Developer with viewer role can view billing charges aligning with the principle of least privileges.

18. **B** (Enable Flow Logs.)
Explanation:
VPC Flow logs track all the network flows and need to be enabled.

19. **B** (Use Managed instance groups across multiple zones.)
Explanation:
It would provide a highly available solution in case a zone went down and managed instance groups would provide the scalability.

20. **A** (gcloud compute instances create "preempt" --preemptible --no-boot-disk-auto-delete.)
Explanation:
The pre-emptible instances need to be created you need to pass the –pre-emptible flag and as disk contents need not be deleted, --no-boot-disk-auto-delete flag needs to be passed.

21. **B** (Set content-type as object metadata to application/pdf on the files.)
Explanation:
The browser needs the correct content-type to be able to interpret and render the file correctly. The content-type can be set on object metadata and should be set to application/pdf.

22. **B** (Go to the Billing page; view the list of projects; find the project in question and select Change billing account; select the correct billing account and save.)
Explanation:
For changing the billing account, you have to select the project and change the billing account.

23. **C** (Delete archived objects older than 30 days and move objects to Coldline Storage after 365 days if the storage class in Multi-regional.)

Answers

Explanation:
The first rule will delete any object if it exceeds from 30 days and is not live (not the latest version). The second rule will change the storage class of the live object from multi-regional to Coldline for objects with age over 365 days.

24. **A** (Generate a Windows password in the console, then use a client capable of communicating via RDP and provide the credentials.)

Explanation:
Connecting to Windows instance involves the installation of the RDP client. GCP does not provide RDP client, and it needs to be installed. Generate Windows instance password to connect to the instance.

25. **B** (Enable the API in the Console.)

Explanation:
The easiest way to enable an API for the project is by using the GCP console.

26. **B** (Create a Failover replica in the same region different zone.)

Explanation:
Failover replica helps provides High Availability for Cloud SQL. The failover replica should be in the same region as the primary instance.

27. **B** (SSH would be allowed as the allow rule overrides the deny.)

Explanation:
The firewall rules are applied according to the priority. And as the allow rule has a higher priority as compared to the deny rule, the SSH access is allowed.

28. **D** (Create a lifecycle policy to switch the objects older than a week to Nearline storage.)

Explanation:
The files are required for a week and then would be needed for only once in month access, Nearline storage would be ideal storage to save cost. The transition of the object can be handled easily using Object Lifecycle Management.

29. **C** (Coldline.)

Answers

E (Multi-Regional.)
Explanation:
Multi-Regional and Coldline storage classes provide multi-region geo-redundant deployment, which can sustain regional failure.

30. **A** (Use the GCP Console, IAM section to view the information.)
Explanation:

The GCP console area is used to view permission assigned to a custom role in a particular project.

31. **B** (Deployment Manager.)
Explanation:
Deployment Manager provides infrastructure as the code capability.

32. **B** (Export audit logs to Cloud Storage via an export sink.)
    D (Create account for auditors to have view access to export storage bucket with the Storage Object Viewer role.)
Explanation:
B and D are the best approaches for providing long term access with least privilege would be to store the data in Cloud Storage and provide the Storage Object viewer role.

33. **B** (10.0.0.0/8)
Explanation:
You can assign standard private CIDR blocks (192.168.0.0/16, 172.16.0.0/12, 10.0.0.0/8) to VPC and their subnets as the IP address range of a VPC.

34. **B** (In the Google Cloud Platform Console, go to the IAM page for your project and apply for the filter "Role: Owner.")
Explanation:
Option B shows you the Owners of the project.

35. **A** (Write a lifecycle management rule in JSON and push it to the bucket with gsutil.)
Explanation:

Answers

Object lifecycle in Cloud Storage can be automatically controlled using a JSON document defining the rules.

36. **A** (SSL Proxy.)
Explanation:
SSL proxy supports TCP traffic and capable of SSL offload.

37. **C** (Enable node auto-upgrades.)
Explanation:
The Kubernetes cluster can be configured for node auto-upgrades to update them to the least stable version of Kubernetes.

38. **C** (In Google Cloud Storage and stored in a Nearline bucket. Set an Object Lifecycle Management policy to delete data older than five years.)
Explanation:
The access pattern fits Nearline storage class requirements, and Nearline is a more cost-effective storage approach than Multi-Regional. The object lifecycle management policy to delete data is correct versus changing the storage class to Coldline as the data is no longer needed.

39. **D** (Deploy the update as a new version. Migrate traffic from the current version to the new version.)
Explanation:
The deployment can be done seamlessly by deploying a new version and migrating the traffic gradually from the older version to the newer version. If any issue is encountered, the traffic can be migrated 100% to the old version.

40. **C** (Use the pricing calculator for App Engine to get an accurate estimation of the expected charges.)
Explanation:
This is the correct way to estimate the charges.

41. **D** (Deploy a new version of the application, and use traffic splitting to send a small percentage of traffic to it.)
Explanation:

Answers

As deploying a new version without assigning it as the default version will not create downtime for the application. Using traffic splitting allows for easily redirecting a small amount of traffic to the new version and can also be quickly reverted without application downtime.

42. **B** (Cloud SQL.)

    C (Cloud Spanner.)

Explanation:
As per GCP documentation, Cloud SQL and Cloud Spanner are relational and transactional database.

43. **A** (Create a cluster on Kubernetes Engine and enable autoscaling on Kubernetes Engine.)

Explanation:
Kubernetes cluster provides auto-scaling feature which can be enabled on the cluster engine.

44. **A** (gcloud container clusters create project-1-cluster --num-nodes 3.)

Explanation:
Kubernetes cluster can be created using the gcloud command only, with the cluster name and --num-nodes parameter.

45. **A** (Create a subnet with a CIDR range of 10.28.0.0/28. Reserve a static internal IP address of 10.28.0.10. Assign the static address to the license server instance.)

Explanation:
The IP is internal; it can be reserved using the static internal IP address, which blocks it and prevents it from getting allocated to another resource.

46. **A** (Add all of the keys into a file that's formatted according to the requirements. Use the gcloud compute instances add-metadata command to upload the keys to each instance.)

Explanation:
Instance-specific SSH keys can help provide users access to the specific bastion host. The keys can be added or removed using the instance metadata.

47. **D** (Give Bob Compute Engine Instance Admin Role for Project A.)

Answers

Explanation:
The access needs to be given only to create instances; the user should be given compute instance admin role, which provides the least privilege.

48. **C** (App Engine Deployer.)
Explanation:
App Engine Deployer permit write access only to create a new version.

49. **D** (Use the gcloud iam roles copy command and set the destination project.)
Explanation:
Cloud SDK "gcloud iam roles copy" can be used to copy the roles to multiple organization or project.

50. **D** (App Engine Standard Environment.)
Explanation:
App Engine Standard Environment provides rapid scaling as compared to App Engine Flexible Environment and is ideal for applications requiring quick start times and handle sudden and extreme spikes.

51. **C** (Using composite objects and parallel uploads to upload the file to Cloud Storage quickly. Then generate a signed URL and securely share it with the contractors.)
Explanation:
As a parallel composite upload, the Cloud Storage file could be quickly uploaded. Signed URLs can be used to share the files with third parties quickly and securely. Signed URLs provide a way for anyone who has the URL to access read or write in time irrespective of having a Google Account.

52. **D** (Google Compute Engine managed instance groups with auto-scaling.)
Explanation:
As an instance group managed by Google Compute Engine, testing can help reduce the time needed for testing. When additional computer resources are required for your application, managed groups of instances can scale the number of cases in the group automatically.

Answers

53. A (Setup the application using App Engine Flexible environment with Cloud VPN to connect to the database)

Explanation:

With Google App Engine you can provide the connectivity to on-premises via Cloud VPN.

54. B (Deploy the new version using the no-promote flag. Split the traffic using Cookie)

Explanation:

Since the application needs to be promoted with the parameter —no-promote to avoid 100% traffic in the new version. Use a cookie approach to retain the experience of the User when the application is deployed and tested.

55. B (Cloud Bigtable)

Explanation:

As the most powerful storage option for IOT and time series data is Cloud Bigtable. A quick, fully managed, highly-scalable NoSQL database service is Google Cloud Bigtable. It is intended for data from 1 TB to hundreds of PB collection and retention processes.

56. A (Cloud Bigtable)

Explanation:

For low latency and high throughput data processing, Cloud Bigtable is ideal storage with analytics.

57. D (Run gcloud config list to check for the project)

Explanation:

With the command gcloud config list you can view the details of the project where you will find the project in which your project is deployed.

58. C (roles/spanner.databaseUser)

Explanation:

It is a machine only roles and provides the ability to read and write to a database; this is the least privilege role to view and edit CloudSpanner tables.

59. D (Use Google Cloud Regional Storage for the first 30 days, and then move to Coldline Storage)

Explanation:

Answers

With frequently accessed data within 30 days, the most cost-effective solution for storage and accessing the data is provided with Google Cloud Regional Storage. Google Cloud Coldline Storage provides the most affordable solution for videos older than 30 days because they are not accessible.

60. **B** (In a secret management system)

Explanation:

As the use of credentials in a Secret Management System such as KMS is recommended. Small pieces of sensitive data are often accessible during building or running times in applications. These data pieces are often called secrets. In concepts like configuration files, secrets are more sensitive but generally allow additional data, such as user data, to be available.

61. **C** (Use gcloud config set compute/region europe-west1 to set the default region for future gcloud commands)

Explanation:

This ensures that the region concerned is used if the command parameter is not overwritten. Manually you can choose another area or region by setting those properties locally without updating the metadata server by setting the value on gcloud client "gcloud config compute/region Region."

62. **A** (gcloud container clusters resize ips --node pool 'pri-node-pool' --size 20)

Explanation:

Resize command is used to increase the number of nodes.

"gcloud container cluster resize <cluster name> --node-pool <pool name> --size <number>"

63. **C** (Enable Logging export to Google BigQuery and use ACLs and views to scope the data shared with the auditor)

Explanation:

For analyzing capability, BigQuery is the best storage and on this access control is managed by ACL's to manage permissions on datasets and projects. BigQuery is a petabyte-size data warehouse, with which you can run SQL queries in near-real-time over large amounts of data.

Answers

64. **B** (Set allUsers to have the Storage Object Viewer role)

Explanation:

You can either public all the files in your bucket or set individual objects for access via your website. In general, it is easier and faster to make all files accessible in your bucket. You can share a bucket by allowing all Users to access the Storage Object Viewer.

65. **D** (Use multi-threaded uploads using the -m option.)

Explanation:

As gsutil, they provide composition objects or parallel uploads to deal with larger files uploads. The gsutil utility can also use object composition automatically in order to upload large, local files to Cloud Storage in parallel. It divides the large file into parts and loads it parallel, and then recomposes it once it is in the cloud (and removes the temporary components locally created). You can activate that by setting' parallel composite upload threshold' on gsutil (or, as the console output suggests, updating your.boto file).

66. **B** (Meet with the cloud operations team and the engineer to discuss load balancer options.)

Explanation:

WebSocket traffic is handled natively by the HTTP(S) load balancer. For back ends that use WebSocket, the load balancer can be used as a front end for scale and availability to communicate with customers. The WebSocket protocol is supported by HTTP(s) Load Balancing. The load balancer requires no additional proxy WebSocket connections configuration.

67. **A** (Apply a network tag of "dev-ssh" to the instance you're trying to connect into and test again.)

Explanation:

Because for instance the firewall needs to be linked to follow the firewall rules. The association can be carried out via the instance using the network tag "dev-ssh." Network tags are attributed to the VM instances of Compute Engine. Tags enable you to make firewall rules and routes for specific VM instances applicable.

68. **C** (Org viewer, project viewer)

Explanation:

Answers

As the Security team of the company wants to only view projects so assign project viewer role as it is the least privilege.

69. A (Use bq query --dry_run to determine the number of bytes read by the query. Use this number in the Pricing Calculator)

Explanation:

To find the estimated cost of BigQuery you need to identify the number of reads, so use dry run parameter which gives you a number of reads then apply it GCP pricing calculator.

70. C (gcloud deployment-manager deployments update)

Explanation:

You can update it as your app or service changes after you have created a deployment. To update an installation using the Deployment Manager: Add or remove resources from an installation. Updating the characteristics of existing deployment resources.

So you can use "deployment-manger deployments update" to update existing deployment.

71. B (In 2 days when you'll hit your billing threshold)

Explanation:

Whichever comes first, because the billing shall be either monthly or the threshold. As with $50 a day and 18 days gone, the threshold of $1000 would hit the bill in 2 days.

72. A (Enable Binary logging and backups for the instance)

Explanation:

Point-in-time recovery allows you to recover an instance at a given time. You can never make a point-in-time recovery to an existing instance. Binary logging and backup are enabled for instance, using on time binary logs from the last backup before the event you want to recover. You can always use a point-in-time retrieve instance.

73. C (Add all of the keys into a file that's formatted according to the requirements. Use the gcloud compute project-info add-metadata command to upload the keys.)

Explanation:

Answers

As wide project SSH keys, access to all instances can assist users. Using the instance metadata, keys can be added or removed. To give users general access to a Linux instance, use project-wide public SSH keys. Public SSH keys project-wide give users access to all of the Linux instances in a project that permits public SSH keys across the entire project. If an instance blocks public SSH keys across the project, a user can not connect to the install by using his project-wide public SSH key unless a single public SSH key is added into the instance metadata.

74. **A** (Store the credentials in a Secret)

Explanation:

Kubernetes offers the secret resource type to store and use credentials in GKE applications directly within the container cluster. Kubernetes secrets objects allow sensitive information such as passwords, OAuth tokens, and the ssh keys to be stored and managed.

75. **B** (Nearline)
    E (Multi-Regional)

Explanation:

as a geo-redundant multi-region storage class, and as a near-line storage class, this may sustain regional failure. The geo-redundancy of the near-line data is determined based on the location type: near-line savings are redundant across multiple regions, providing a better availability than nearby data stored at regional locations. The geo-redundancy of close-line data is based on location type: It also ensures maximum data availability, even in the event of a major disruption.

76. **A** (SSH would be denied as the deny rule overrides the allow)

Explanation:

The SSH access is denied because of the priority application of the firewall rules, and the higher priority of a deny rule than the permit rule. The priority of the firewall rule is an integer between 0 and 65535. Lower numbers show higher priorities. If you do not prioritize when you create a rule, a priority of 1000 is assigned.

77. **C** (The average CPU for the entire instance group is below 60%.)

Explanation:

Answers

The Auto Scaler checks the average use of the CPU throughout the instances and is not done on a single instance. The average CPU utilization of a managed instance group allows you to scale autoscale. The Autoscaler will collect the CPU use of the instances of the group and determine whether they need to be sized by means of this policy. You set the target CPU usage that the autoscaler should maintain and that level will be maintained by the autoscaler.

78. **B** (In GCP console, click Traffic Splitting and direct 100% of the traffic to the previous version)

Explanation:

To revert back to the previous version of an application click on traffic splitting which moves 100 % of traffic to the previous version. This option is available in the GCP console. Traffic splitting distributes a percentage of traffic to versions of your application.

79. **C** (Billing Account Billing administrator)
    E (Project Owner)

Explanation:

You must be a project owner and billing administrator on the destination billing account to change the billing account for an existing project.

80. **B** (Grant no Google Cloud Identity and Access Management (Cloud IAM) roles to users, and use granular ACLs on the bucket.)

Explanation:

Because this gives the least privilege needed to access data and minimizes the risk of access to incorrect people by accident.

81. **D** (Create a snapshot from the disk. Create a disk from the snapshot in the europe-west2-c zone. Create a new VM with that disk.)

Explanation:

A snapshot and creation of the disk from the snapshot in the zone are the most appropriate way to create a disk replica. Disks are zonal resources, so they reside throughout their lives in a particular area. Drive contents can be moved to a different zone using "—source-snapshot" in the desired zone and create a new disk using "—source-snapshot." The disk contents can also be moved across project or zone, using the creation of an image (using " gcloud compute images create") or by creating a new disk in the desired project and/or zone with the use of "—image."

82. **D** (Create a Cloud Storage lifecycle rule with Age: "30", Storage Class: "Standard", and Action: "Set to Coldline", and create a second GCS life-cycle rule with Age: "365", Storage Class: "Coldline", and Action: "Delete".)

Explanation:

2 actions are necessary. After 30 days the first archival can be done by Coldline's SetStorageClass action. Secondly, delete the information after one year, which can be deleted with 365 days of age. The age is measured in the creation time of the object.

83. **B** (Create a Failover replica in the same region different zone)

Explanation:

High Availability for Cloud SQL is a failover replica that provides help. It must be replicated in the same area as the primary instance. The HA setup, sometimes referred to as a cluster, allows data redundancy. The configuration consists of a principal (master) instance in the primary zone as well as a secondary area failover replica. By semi-synchronous replication, any modification in the data and user tables of the primary instance is copied to the failover replica. This configuration reduces downtime, and your data is still available for client applications in case of an instance or area failure.

84. **A** (Cloud Functions)

Explanation:

The Google Cloud Function is a cloud-building, serverless execution environment. You write simple, one-two functions for events issued from your cloud infrastructure and services with cloud functions. You can use them. When an event is being watched, your function is triggered. In a fully managed environment, your code is implemented. No infrastructure needs to be provided, or any servers need to be managed. Cloud Functions can help automatically scale as per the demand, with no invocations if no demand.

85. **B** (Install with Cloud Launcher)

Explanation:

GCP provides Cloud Launcher from market place which is ready to go deployment stack solution for the requirement.

Answers

86. **D** (Create a new Google Group and add all users to the group. Use gcloud projects add-iam-policy-binding with the Project Viewer role and Group email address.)

Explanation:

Whenever possible use Google groups with appropriate role linked to project.

87. **A** (Create a subnet with a CIDR range of 10.28.0.0/28. Reserve a static internal IP address of 10.28.0.10. Assign the static address to the license server instance.)

Explanation:

Since the IP is internal, a static internal IP address can reserve it, which blocks it and prevents the IP being allocated to a different resource.

88. **C** (Create a custom counter logging metric that uses a regex to extract the data format into a label. At the end of the month, use the metric viewer to see the group by the label.)

Explanation:

Log-based metrics on the logs already logged may be created as defined by the custom user. At the end of the month, these measurements can be used to check API Call statistics by format for details. User-defined (log-based) metrics will be developed by a project user. The number of log entries that correspond in a certain filter is counted, or the values of particular log entries are tracked.

89. **B** (Set the min_idle_instances property in the app.yaml.)

Explanation:

As min idle instances can be set to have minimum idle, always running instances. In min idle instances, the number of instances to keep running and ready for traffic. Note, you will be charged whether or not traffic is received for the number of instances specified. This configuration applies only to the most traffic version. Take into account the following:

The minimal level of run-time support helps you to reduce running costs in idle times but means that fewer instances are immediately available to respond to a sudden load spike. While high minimum helps you to handle the spikes in request load of the application. App Engine maintains the minimum of instances in which incoming requests are fulfilled. You are charged to handle requests for the number of instances specified. To work properly with this feature, you must make sure warm-up requests are enabled, and warm-up requests are processed for your application.

Answers

90. **B** (Ask Auditors to navigate to the IAM page and check member and roles section)
Explanation:
By going to the IAM page, an auditor can review all the members and roles created for the project.

91. **C** (Nearline)
Explanation:
As they want to access data monthly, so the use of Nearline storage is the best choice. Google Cloud Storage Nearline is a low cost, highly durable data storage service. In scenarios where there are a little less accessibility, a 30-day minimum storage time and costs for data access, nearline storage is a better choice than multi-regional storage or regional storage.

92. **C** (roles/storage.admin)
Explanation:
Bucket and objects would be fully controlled by the team members as roles / storage.admin. When a role is applied to a particular bucket, control only applies to the specified bucket and objects in the bucket.

93. **A** (Cloud Storage)
    B (Cloud Spanner)
Explanation:
To store the relational data which is approx. more than 10 TB and need to be spread across the region then use Cloud Spanner while for storing the images use Cloud Storage.

94. **B** (Cloud Storage)
Explanation:
Cloud Storage would be the ideal choice, and the website is static and needs to be hosted with high availability and limited budget.

95. **D** (Using Command line, use the --dry_run option on BigQuery to determine the number of bytes read, and then use the price calculator to determine the cost.)
Explanation:

Answers

The —dry-run option can be used before they are actually fired to price your inquiries. The query returns the read bytes that can be used to estimate the query costs using the price calculator.

96. **A** (Cloud DataStore)

Explanation:

For your web and mobile applications, Cloud Datastore provides a scalable, fully managed NoSQL document database. It is useful for semi-structured application data, hierarchical data and durable for key value data.

97. **D** (gcloud compute firewall-rules create "open-ssh" --network $NETWORK --allow tcp:22)

Explanation:

With this command, you can create firewall rule in order to allow or deny the traffic. There are a variety of protocols that you can use with this command for connection over that protocol like ssh, tcp, udp, icmp, etc.

98. **C** (kubectl get svc -o jsonpath='{.items[*].status.loadBalancer.ingress[0].ip}')

Explanation:

"kubectl get svc" is used to get the data and jsonpath is used to parse the data.

99. **B** (Managed Instance Group on Compute Engine) and **D** (HTTP Load Balancer)

Explanation:

HTTP(S) load balancing can balance HTTP and HTTPS traffic across multiple backend instances, across multiple regions. Your entire app is available via a single global IP address, resulting in a simplified DNS setup. Load Balancing HTTP(S) is scalable, fault tolerant, does not require pre-warming and allows load balancing based on the contents. It provides SSL ending and loads balancing for HTTPS traffic. The custom Linux distribution is supported only by the compute engine.

100. **A** (Coldline)

Explanation:

As the data is rarely accessed and only access in case of disaster recovery then Coldline storage is ideal for that.

101. **C** (Configure read replicas)

Answers

Explanation
Read replicas can help to manage the read traffic reducing the load from the primary database.

102. **C** (roles/bigquery.dataViewer and roles/bigquery.jobUser)

Explanation
roles/bigquery.dataViewer and roles/bigquery.jobUser provide the user requirement to only query the data, they should have access to view the dataset and query the dataset.
All other roles provide more than required privileges.

103. **A** (Your managed instance group's health check is repeatedly failing, either to a misconfigured health check or misconfigured firewall rules not allowing the health check to access the instances.)

Explanation
If the health check fails either because the application is not configured properly, or because of instances in which the firewall does not allow health checks, instances (normal or preemptible) would be terminated and relaunched.

104. **C** (Export the data for the billing account(s) involved to BigQuery; then use BigQuery to analyze the service data for the desired projects, by day and month.)

Explanation
Billing data are available for export to BigQuery for daily and monthly calculation of service expenditure.

105. **A** (HTTPS Load Balancer)

Explanation
The HTTPS load balancer provides SSL termination feature support for HTTPS traffic. SSL proxy is not recommended for HTTPS traffic. SSL termination is not supported by HTTP load balancer. SSL offload is noy supported by TCP proxy and TCP proxy is also not recommended for HTTPS traffic.

106. **C** (gsutil mb -c coldline gs://archive_bucket)

Explanation
Coldline is used when data is unusual (i.e. only once a year) to access. This is typically for disaster recovery or archived data which may or may not be necessary some time in the future.

Answers

107. **A (gcloud compute images list)**

Explanation

Family names are image attributes therefore gcloud compute image list is used to determine family names.

108. **A (gcloud components list)**

Explanation

"gcloud components list" is used to view the components list with the installation status. "gcloud component list" is an invalid command and rest of the two commands help to view and edit Cloud SDK properties and does not provide the component details.

109. **D (Create a lifecycle policy to delete the objects older than a month.)**

Explanation

The files can be deleted as they are no longer needed and do not need to be stored. Object Lifecycle Management can easily handle the transition of the object.

110. **B (Use the Rolling Update feature to deploy/roll back versions with different managed instance group templates.)**

Explanation

Rolling update helps to apply the update to a controlled number of instances in order to maintain high availability and rollback capability in the event of problems. Therefore, option B is correct. Options A, C, and D are wrong because scaling is to create stateless, disposable VMs able to scale and deploy seamlessly.

111. **D (Deploy a new version of the application but use traffic splitting to only direct a small number of users to the new version.)**

Explanation

Applying this option will not create downtime for the application by deploying a new version without assigning it as the default version. Using traffic splitting allows a small amount of traffic to be easily redirected to the new version and can also be reversed quickly without downtime for the application.

112. **C (A multi-regional Cloud Storage bucket)**

Explanation

Answers

The key storage needs are global, enabling lifecycle management and capacity sharing. Cloud Storage is best solution as it can be configured multi-regional, have lifecycle management rules for automatic deletion after 30 days and files sharing with others. Whereas Datastore is not ideal for unstructured data and is a NoSQL solution, Disks are regional and not ideal for storage options for content sharing, and SSD disks are an ephemeral virtual machine storage option.

113. **B** (Deploy the monitoring pod as a DaemonSet)

Explanation

Daemon set is used to deploy applications or tools that you need to run on all the nodes. DaemonSets are useful to deploy ongoing background tasks that you need to run on all or some nodes without user intervention. Option A is not a viable option. Option C is incorrect because Stateful set is used to maintain state and option D is wrong because pods cannot be controlled by Deployment manager.

114. **B** (Create a new service account and key with the required limited permissions. Set the instance to use the new service account. Edit the code to use the service account key)

Explanation

Service accounts are the best option to provide particular acces to the application. A service account is part of your application or a virtual machine (VM) rather than an individual end user. Your application assumes the service account identity to call Google APIs in order not to involve users directly.

115. **B** (Load data into Google BigQuery)

Explanation

BigQuery is the only one of these Google products that supports an SQL interface and a sufficiently high SLA (99.9 %) for easy access.
Multi petabyte data is not supported by Cloud SQL
SQL interface is not provide by Cloud Storage
Datastore does not support SQL interface and it is a noSQL solution.

116. **D** (Coldline)

Explanation

Coldline storage is the best and cheap solution for infrequently access archive data. Google Cloud Storage Coldline is a cost-effective, highly durable data archiving, online

Answers

backup, and disaster recovery storage service. Your data is available within milliseconds, not hours or days, unlike other cold storage services. Other options are not suitable for archival data.

117. **C** (Enable object versioning on the website's static data files stored in Google Cloud Storage.)

Explanation

Option C is the correct answer as this is a seamless way to ensure the last known good version of the static content is always available.

Option A is incorrect because this approach does not scale well, there is a lot of management work involved.

Option B is wrong because this would add a lot of overhead to the process and cause conflicts between different deployments of the Deployment Manager that could lead to unexpected behavior if an old version is changed.

Option D is wrong because this process of copying is unreliable and makes it difficult to keep things in sync, as well as not providing a way to rollback once a bad version of the data has been written to the copy.

118. **C** (Use "gcloud config set project" to set the default project)

Explanation

Option C is correct because to manage the config / default you need to use gcloud.

Option A and D are wrong because entering this command will not achieve the desired outcome and will cause an error.

Option B is wrong because the gcloud configuration settings are assumed by the bq command-line tool and can not be set by BigQuery.

119. **A** (Use docker to create a container image, push it to the Google Container Registry, deploy the uploaded image to Kubernetes with kubectl)

Explanation

To package and deploy your application on GKE, you must:
1. Package your app into a Docker image
2. Run the container locally on your machine (optional)
3. Upload the image to a registry
4. Create a container cluster
5. Deploy your app to the cluster
6. Expose your app to the Internet

Answers

7. Scale up your deployment
8. Deploy a new version of your app

120. **D** (gsutil mb -c nearline gs://archive_bucket)

Explanation

Nearline-Data that you do not expect to frequently access (i.e. not more than once a month). Ideal for backup and multimedia content serving long-tail. Therefore, Nearline is an ideal storage class as the data needs to be accessed on monthly basis. Also gsutil needs -c parameter to pass the class.

121. **A** (Enable auto-healing for the managed instance groups)

Explanation

Autohealing policy based on an application-based health check that periodically checks that your application responds as expected in each instance of the MIG. If an application does not respond to an instance, the instance will be recreated automatically. It is more accurate to check that an application responds than just verifying that an instance is up and running.

122. **C** (Create a subnet with a CIDR range of 10.28.0.0/28. Reserve a static internal IP address of 10.28.0.10. Assign the static address to the license server instance.)

Explanation

Only the 10.28.0.0/28 CIDR range would include the address of 10.28.0.10. It has 16 ip addresses, i.e. from 10.28.0.0 to 10.28.0.15

123. **B** (Use the appropriate pre-defined IAM roles for each of the access levels needed for Cloud Storage and BigQuery. Add your users to those roles for each of the services.)

Explanation

Google's best practice is to use predefined rules on custom and primitive legacy roles. Predefined roles can assist in providing fine grain control per service. When predefined roles are not available then user should use custom roles. Primitive roles are project or service resource levels and it is not recommended by Google that if they do not allow fine grained access control.

Answers

124. **B** (Delete archived objects older than 30 days and move objects to Coldline Storage after 365 days if the storage class in Multi-regional.)

Explanation

First rule will remove any object if it is over 30 days of age and not live (not the latest version). Second rule for objects over 365 days of age will change the storage class of the live object from multi-regional to Coldline.

125. **C** (Generate Windows password. Check security group for 3389 firewall rule. Install RDP Client to connect)

Explanation

Connecting to the Windows instance requires RDP client installation. GCP does not provide the RDP client and it needs to be installed. Generate password for Windows instance for connecting to instance and the RDP port is 3389.
Option B and D are wrong because external client and direct connection to GCP console is required.
Options A and B are wrong because port 22 is SSH

126. **A** (Move objects to Coldline Storage after 365 days if the storage class in Multi-regional First rule has no effect on the bucket.)

Explanation

First rule will remove any object if it is over 30 days of age and not live (not the latest version). Second rule for objects over 365 days of age will change the storage class of the live object from multi-regional to Coldline.

127. **B** (Cloud Pub/Sub, Cloud Dataflow, BigQuery)

Explanation

The need for ingestion, transformation and storage of Cloud Pub / Sub, Cloud Dataflow, BigQuery is the ideal stack for IoT data management.

128. **B** (Perform the health check using HTTP by hosting a basic web server)

Explanation

Network Load Balancer does not support TCP health checks, so it is necessary to carry out HTTP health checks. For health checks, you can run a basic web server for each instance.

Answers

129. **A (Enable auto-repairing for the nodes)**

Explanation

The node auto-repair feature, which would allow Kubernetes engine to replace unhealthy nodes, could increase resilience and high availability.

Option B is wrong because there is no auto-healing feature for nodes

Option C is wrong because auto-upgrades is used for node version upgradation to the latest stable Kubernetes version.

Option D is not applicable for Kubernete cluster

130. **D (Create a budget alert for desired percentages such as 50%, 90%, and 100% of your total monthly budget.)**

Explanation

You can apply budget alerts to either a billing account or a project and you can set the budget alert to a specific amount or match it to the expenditure of the previous month. When expenditure exceeds a percentage of your budget, the alerts will be sent to billing administrators and billing account users.

Option A is incorrect because there are no budget settings in App Engine

Option B is wrong because it will not trigger automatic alerts

Option C is wrong as Linked cards does not alert

131. **A (Assign roles/bigquery.dataViewer and roles/bigquery.jobUser roles to a group; add users to groups)**

Explanation

These two roles are required To access and query the least privileged BigQuery tables inline. Google's best practices recommend using predefined roles and setting up groups to monitor multiple users with the same responsibility

132. **C (In Google Cloud Storage and stored in a Nearline bucket. Set an Object Lifecycle Management policy to change the storage class to Coldline for data older than 5 years.)**

Explanation

Access pattern fits the requirements of Nearline storage class and Nearline is more cost-effective than Multi-Regional storage approach. The object lifecycle management policy is ideal for archiving to move data to Coldline.

Answers

133. **D** (Create a Service of type ClusterIP for Deployment A. Have Deployment B use the Service IP address.)

Explanation

Option D will expose the service to an internal IP address of the cluster. By selecting this method, the service is only accessible within the cluster.
Option A is wrong because the service is exposed externally using the load balancer of a cloud provider, and Ingress can only work with nodeport, not LoadBalancer.
Option B is wrong as this exposes Deployment A over the public internet.
Option C is wrong as LoadBalancer will expose the service publicly.

134. **A** (NoSQL)

Explanation

NoSQL such as Bigtable and Datastore is an ideal solution for storing sensor ID and various discrete information items. It also offers the ability to connect with other data. It is also possible to configure Datastore to store data in multi-region locations.

135. **C** (The kubeconfig is missing the credentials. Run the gcloud container clusters get-credentials command.)

Explanation

This command is used to set context whenever connection is refused.

136. **D** (Set automaticRestart availability policy to true)

Explanation

automaticRestart Availability Policy specifies how the instance reacts to the crashes and termination of the system and should be set to true to restart.

137. **A** (Update the existing Container Engine cluster with the following command: gcloud alpha container clusters update mycluster --enable-autoscaling --min-nodes=1 --max-nodes=10)

Explanation

You need to update your cluster to allow min and max node auto scaling to scale as required.
Option B is wrong because you donot have to create a new cluster and you can update the existing cluster to allow auto scaling.
Option C is wrong as the cluster needs to updated and not the instances.
Option D is wrong as it would only increase the nodes.

Answers

138. **B** (Configure Stackdriver Monitoring for all Projects, and export to BigQuery)
Explanation
Stackdriver monitoring metrics can be exported to either BigQuery or Google Cloud Storage. BigQuery, however, is a better option for future analysis.
Option A is wrong because project logs are maintained in Stackdriver and its data retention capability is limited.
Option B is wrong as Google Cloud Storage does not support analytics capability.
Option D is wrong as Stackdriver cannot retain data for 5 year.

139. **B** (gcloud functions deploy)
Explanation
gcloud functions deploy command is used to deploy code in Google.

140. **C** (Create the query and use the --dry_run option to determine the amount of data read, and then use the price calculator to determine the cost.)
Explanation
You can use the —dry-run option to price your query before it's actually fired. The Query returns the read bytes, which can then be used to estimate the cost of the query with the Pricing Calculator.

141. **C** (Create a new node pool in the same cluster, and migrate the workload to the new pool.)
Explanation
The cluster machine type can not be changed by using commands. It is necessary to create a new node pool with the updated machine type and migrate the workload to the new node pool.

142. **A** (Run your script on a new virtual machine with the BigQuery access scope enabled)
Explanation
To create a service account with the BigQuery access is the recommended approach
Option B is wrong because you need to use the user's private key and recommendation for its use is from on-site or other cloud platforms
Option C is wrong because the bq command is not required with the python client and it is installed by default . It is for direct interaction with BigQuery on the command line.

Answers

Option D is wrong because it is a BigQuery connectivity issue and not a mismatch issue for the client version.

143. **D** (Use the gcloud compute instances add-metadata [INSTANCE_NAME] --metadata block-project-ssh-keys=TRUE command to block the access

Explanation

The project wide SSH access can be blocked by using –metadata block- project –ssh –keys =TRUE

144. **A** (For your organization, in the Google Cloud Platform Console under Roles, select both roles and combine them into a new custom role.)

Explanation

Option A is right because this will create new role on the organization level with combined permissions

145. **B** (Perform app engine deploy using the --project parameter)

Explanation

gcloud app deploy permits the --project to be passed to override the project that the App Engine want to deploy.

146. **D** (Use "gcloud container clusters resize" with the desired number of nodes.)

Explanation

this command can be used to resize the Kubernetes cluster

147. **B** (Revoke the key, remove the key from Git, purge the Git history to remove all traces of the file, ensure the key is added to the .gitignore file.)

Explanation

All key traces have to be removed and the key has to be added to the.gitignore file therefore option B is correct.

148. **A** (Load logs into Google BigQuery.)
     B (Upload log files into Google Cloud Storage.)

Explanation

Google Cloud Storage can provide archival options for the long term, and BigQuery provides analytics capabilities.

Answers

149. D (~/bin)
Explanation
Option D is correct because only HOME directory is persisted across sessions.

150. C (Use Deployment Manager Preview feature)
Explanation
Deployment Manager provides the feature of the preview to check which resources are to be created.

151. A (Create a new Service that points to the existing deployment.)
Explanation:
Service is how we expose the deployments. It is a persistent endpoint that we can interact with, and it will send the traffic over to the pods inside the deployment.

152. D (gcloud compute images list.)
Explanation:
Family names are an attribute of images. This would list all the images and their family names.

153. D (Enable the automatic node upgrades setting.)
Explanation:
In UI this is only a checkbox. In CLI, you can use --enable-autoupgrade.

154. D (The average CPU for the entire instance group is below 60%.)
Explanation:
The autoscaler averages the CPU utilization of the entire group. So one instance could be higher than the usage threshold.

155. C (Put the data on Cloud Storage and generate a signed URL that will expire in one hour, and securely share the URL.)
Explanation:
A signed URL is a URL which provides permission up to some extent and time to make a request. Put the data on the Cloud Storage and generate a signed URL which will expire in one hour, and share the URL securely.

Answers

156. **C (Cloud Storage.)**
Explanation:
Cloud Storage allows the storage and retrieval of any amount of data at any time. You can use Cloud Storage for a variety of scenarios which includes serving website content, distributing large data objects to users through direct download or storing data for archival and disaster recovery.

157. **C (Deploy the monitoring pod as a DaemonSet.)**
Explanation:
A DaemonSet makes sure that all or maybe some Nodes run a copy of a Pod. When the nodes are added to the cluster, Pods are added to them. As nodes are removed from the cluster, those Pods are removed. Deleting a DaemonSet will clean up the Pods it created.

158. **C (Enable Binary Logging.)**
Explanation:
The binary log is described as a set of log files which contain all the information about data modifications made to a MySQL server instance. The log is enabled by initializing the server using the --log-bin option. The binary log was introduced in MySQL 3.23.14. It contains all statements that are used to update the data.

159. **B (Enable the API in the Console.)**
Explanation:
API Enabling is associated with the current project, and adds the monitoring pages, and enables billing for the API if billing is enabled for the project.

160. **B (Use an App Engine Flexible Environment.)**
Explanation:
Flexible environments can use a Dockerfile to create custom runtimes. They specifically run on port 8080.

161. **A (Enable Flow Logs.)**
Explanation:
Using flow logs saves networking traffic to the logs, though it does generate a lot of data.

Answers

162. **D** (Set the Content-Type metadata for the object to "application/pdf.")

Explanation:

The commonly set metadata is Content-Type (known as MIME type) that allows the browsers to render the object efficiently. All objects have a value which is specified in their Content-Type metadata, but this value does not have to match with the underlying type of the object

163. **A** (The kubeconfig is missing the credentials. Run the *gcloud container clusters get-credentials* command.)

Explanation:

Kubectl does not know about a cluster. Using this command, you can get the cluster credentials and save them locally.

164. **A** (When creating the instance template use the startup script metadata key to bootstrap the application.)

Explanation:

The startup script is a simple way to get your application bootstrapped without using any additional tools.

165. **D** (Change the IP address range in the filter to only allow known IP addresses.)

Explanation:

By using 0.0.0.0/0, you are opening the port to the internet. By allowing known IP addresses, it will not block anyone on the list.

166. **D** (Have Pub/Sub push messages to a Cloud Function.)

Explanation:

A publisher application creates and sends a message to a Pub/Subtopic. Cloud Pub/Sub offers message delivery and best-effort ordering to existing subscribers.

167. **A** (Edit the number of replicas in the YAML file and rerun the *kubectl apply.*)

Explanation:

If you create a deployment with the kubectl create or apply commands, then you can update with *kubectl apply -f file.yaml.*

Answers

168. **D** (Use docker to create a container image, push it to the Google Container Registry, deploy the uploaded image to Kubernetes with *kubectl.*)

Explanation:

Kubernetes works with container images, not Dockerfiles, and the images need to be in an accessible Container Registry.

169. **A** (Create a service account, grant it the least visible privileges to the required services, generate and download a key. Use the key to authenticate inside the application.)

Explanation:

A service account is a special account which can be used by applications and services working on Compute Engine instance to interact with other GCP APIs. Applications use service account credentials to authorize themselves. Credentials can be used to perform actions within the permissions granted by the service account and virtual machine instance

170. **A** (gcloud container clusters create Linux-academy-dev-cluster --num-nodes 4.)

Explanation:

gcloud container clusters create - create a cluster for running containers.

171. **D** (Apply a network tag of "dev-ssh" to the instance you're trying to connect into and test again.)

Explanation:

A target tag looks for instances with a matching network tag. If you haven't applied the tag to the network, you'll be unable to connect, unless another rule opens the port.

172. **A** (Create a custom counter logging metric that uses a regex to extract the data format into a label. At the end of the month, use the metric viewer to see the group by the label.)

Explanation:

This is a simple solution that only requires the metric to be created, and then Stackdriver will track each occurrence.

173. **B** (Use the *gcloud compute ssh* command.)

Explanation:

Answers

gcloud compute ssh command takes care of authentication and the translation of the instance name into an IP address.

174. **B** (Each log sink destination has its time window for saving the data.)

Explanation:

Cloud Storage takes some time to persist the data. And each log sink destination takes some time for saving the data.

175. **A** (You must make sure that the appropriate GPU driver is installed.)
    B (You must select which boot disk image you want to use for the instance.)

Explanation:

Before creating an instance with a GPU, you must select your boot instance and install the needed GPU driver.

176. **A** (gcloud config list)

Explanation:

The gcloud config list command in SDK lists all active configuration properties. Include the account for allowing Cloud Platform, the current Cloud Platform project, and the default region and area of Compute Engine when set.

177. **B** (gcloud logging)

Explanation:

gcloud logging command is used to manage the stack driver logging.

"gcloud logging GROUP | COMMAND [GCLOUD_WIDE_FLAG ...]"

Here the group is where you define what type of thing you want to manage like log, metrics, sink or resource description. In command, you define either read or write. In GCLOUD_WIDE_FLAG you can define with the account name, configuration, project, etc.

178. **D** (man gcloud_compute_instances_create)

Explanation:

You can connect the component with the groups or commands with underscores in order to directly use the man pages. This would map the command to create instances of gcloud compute.

179. **A** (The alpha component isn't installed.)

Explanation:

Answers

By installing the alpha component, he can run commands in which alpha are added. Otherwise this the type of error you could expect if it is not installed.

180. **C (A Cloud Storage bucket.)**

Explanation:

Cloud Storage is ideal storage for the files that need to be exported. It is the most secure and durable storage. Cloud Storage enables any amount of data to be stored worldwide at any time and recovered.

181. **C (File Export with CSV)**

Explanation:

The easiest and simple way to go for excel file for the report is to export file into CSV format.

182. **B (Use Pub/Sub notifications and listen for messages with a Cloud Function.)**

Explanation:

However, it'll only get notifications using Pub / Sub if they happen. Because alerts are supported and you can execute code in response to alerts using Cloud Function. This would be easy to implement and affordable.

183. **D (Show them how to use the gcloud component of the Cloud SDK.)**

Explanation:

Cloud SDK is a code, and it is documented, that you do not need to develop and maintain. It makes you to just pick your required code and use it. It is easier and reproducible.

184. **B (The project was created by one of the engineers and not attached to the organization.)**

Explanation:

When you create any project, you have an option to attach this project to the organization because the organization is the root resource in the GCP to manage the project. If you do not attach the project to the organization then that user's GCP account when deleted it will automatically delete the project as well.

185. **A (gcloud components list)**

Answers

Explanation:
This command will list all components in Cloud SDK For each component; it lists The status of the component (description), ID (used to refer to the component within other[gcloud components] commands), size of the component.

186. **D (roles/bigquery.dataViewer and roles/bigquery.jobUser)**
Explanation:
dataViewer and job user both have the least privilege capability and have access to run some queries. They have access to list/get projects while in data viewer it has some more access like list tables, get metadata table, get table data, get dataset metadata.

187. **A (Export your audit logs to Cloud Storage and store them for a long period of time.)**
Explanation:
As you want the best practice to store the audit logs securely in Cloud Storage as backed up and saved as long as it is practical.

188. **B (Flow logs)**
Explanation:
Flow log is the feature in networking which helps you to track the data from internal VPC traffic between VPC and on-premises.

189. **D (Add the user inside of G Suite, add them as a member of the project, and grant them the required roles)**
Explanation:
To add new employee you need to add that user in GSuite and also add as the project's member. Also, assign its desired roles to it.

190. **C (Network forensics.)**
Explanation:
Google says their VPC flow logs are intended to promote cases of utilization, such as networking usage and monitoring, network forensics, egress optimization and security analytics, and security analysis in real-time.

Answers

191. **D** (Use the default Compute Engine service account and set its scopes. Let the code find the default service account using "Application Default Credentials")

Explanation:

There is no need to create your own service account if your application is running on Compute Engine, Kubernetes Engine, App Engine Flexible or cloud functions. Compute Engine has an automatically generated default service account for you and, if required, you can assign a different service account. The instance automatically runs as the default service account when you create a new instance and has a set of permissions for authorization.

When you have a service account, ADC is able to find your credentials implicitly without changing the code, ADC will first check whether the GOOGLE APPLICATION CREDENTIALS environment variable is set. When the variable has been set, ADC will utilize the variable's service account file. If no environment variable has been established for applications that run on those services, ADC uses the default service account provided by Compute Engine, Kubernetes Engine, App Engine, and Cloud. If ADC does not use the above credentials, an error occurs.

192. **A** (allAuthenticatedUsers)

Explanation:

This scope is an identifier which represents anyone who is authenticated with a Google account. So in this way you avoid your bucket to be available publically.

193. **A** (Use the gcloud iam roles copy command and set the destination project)

Explanation:

With the "gcloud iam roles copy" command you can easily and fastly copy the roles across the projects.

194. **C** (Predefined Role)

Explanation:
- bigquery.user
- bigquery.jobUser
- bigquery.admin

all of these are pre-defined roles that have multiple permissions on the basis of requirement so use job user role which has the least privilege and has the right to run queries.

Answers

195. **B** (Create a subnet with a CIDR range of 10.28.0.0/28. Reserve a static internal IP address of 10.28.0.10. Assign the static address to the license server instance.)

Explanation:

As we need static internal IP address so we need to create a subnet with CIDR range 10.28.0.0/28 so the given IP address will come in that range as it is larger enough. Then, in the end, assign this static IP address which you reserve to the server instance.

196. **D** (Set the min_idle_instances property in the app.yaml)

Explanation:

With this command, you will allow setting the number of idle instances that will be available for burst traffic.

197. **A** (Install the Stackdriver monitoring and logging agents on the instance)

Explanation:

Only instance based metrics will be logged if you activate stack driver logging. For this to work, the agents must be installed. So you have to install the agent. The agents are aware of how Apache monitors and records data.

198. **C** (Add all of the keys into a file that's formatted according to the requirements. Use the "gcloud compute project-info add-metadata" command to upload the keys.)

Explanation:

"gcloud compute project-info add-metadata" is used to add and update the project-wide metadata. Each instance has access to a server of metadata which can be used to query metadata from the tool. Metadata entries across the project are visible for all instances. So here download keys so that all instances can see it.

199. **A** (Create a service account and JSON key. Use the "gsutil signurl -d 30m " command and pass in the JSON key and bucket)

Explanation:

To set the duration fro sign URL you need to use d parameter in the following command "gsutil signurl –d <duration>."

200. **C** (Both of the Above.)
Explanation:

Answers

GCP documentation states that to help you with the project planning and controlling costs, you can set a budget.

201. **C (Both A and B.)**

Explanation:

The purpose behind creating a budget is that you can trigger alert notifications which are sent to the billing administrators and the billing account users when the costs exceed a percentage of the budget or the amount, which is specified.

202. **A (Three Components.)**

Explanation:

Fundamentally, the data flow is described as taking some data or information and moving it around, processing it in interesting ways and remembering it. We associate these things with three class of services.

203. **C (Both A and B.)**

Explanation:

Moving data could also mean loading some data from disk into memory.

204. **B (Mental Model.)**

Explanation:

A Mental Model is the simplified version of reality, which is used by your mind to anticipate events or conclude them.

205. **D (All of the Above.)**

Explanation:

We associate these things with three classes of service, network service, compute service and storage services.

206. **A (GCP.)**

Explanation:

Answers

Google Cloud Platform (GCP) is a platform of cloud computing services that grew with the Google App Engine framework which is used for hosting web applications from Google's data centers.

207. **D (All of the Above.)**

Explanation:

Compute Engine in Compute products are described as Virtual Machines, disks, and networks. This is the most relatable Google Cloud Product, just like computers you might buy from stores, you can run whatever you want to run, and perform virtually anything you want to perform.

208. **D (All of the Above.)**

Explanation:

Each GCP project contains:
- A project name
- A project ID
- A project number

209. **A (Event-driven server less function.)**

Explanation:

Cloud Function which is a little way down in the list describes as Event-driven server less function. Cloud Function even performs faster than the Compute Engine within the 10th of the second and manages all the scaling for you, automatically.

210. **C (AI and Machine Learning Section.)**

Explanation:

The Cloud TPU is enlisted in AI and Machine Learning sections, but it is a specialized hardware for Machine Learning (ML), so it is kind of like a Compute Engine Instance, but this one is built for Tensor Flow Processing instead of General-Purpose Processing. TPU stands for Tensor Flow Processing Unit.

211. **A (BigQuery.)**

Explanation:

Your billing data can be accessed through BigQuery.

Answers

212.   **A (True.)**

Explanation:

Setting a budget lets you track how your cost is growing towards that amount. You can apply a budget to either a billing account or a project, and you can set the budget at a specific amount or match it to the previous month's cost.

213.   **A (Administrator Account.)**

Explanation:

Each user has a quota of how many projects he can afford and your billing account has a separate quota of how many projects are linked to the billing account. Google automatically creates a project for your administrator account.

About Our Products

Other products from IPSpecialist LTD regarding Cloud technology are:

- AWS Certified Cloud Practitioner Technology Workbook

- AWS Certified Solutions Architect - Associate Technology Workbook

- AWS Certified Developer - Associate Technology Workbook

- AWS Certified SysOps Administrator – Associate Technology Workbook

- AWS Certified DevOps Engineer - Professional Technology Workbook

- AWS Certified Solution Architect - Professional Technology Workbook

- AWS Certified Advanced Networking – Specialty Technology Workbook

- AWS Certified Big Data – Specialty Technology Workbook

- AWS Certified Security – Specialty Technology Workbook

Upcoming products from IPSpecialist LTD regarding GCP technology are:

About Our Products

- Google Certified Professional Cloud Architect Technology Workbook

- Google Certified Professioanl Data Engineer Technology Workbook

About Our Products

Note from the Author:

Reviews are gold to authors! If you have enjoyed this book and it helped you along certification, would you consider rating it and reviewing it?

Link to Product Page:

Made in the USA
Middletown, DE
12 September 2019